A Mathematician Reveals How the Secrets of
Decision Theory Can Help You Make the
Right Decision *Every Time*

the > Right
Decision

JAMES STEIN, Ph.D.

New York   Chicago   San Francisco   Lisbon   London   Madrid   Mexico City
Milan   New Delhi   San Juan   Seoul   Singapore   Sydney   Toronto

Library of Congress Cataloging-in-Publication Data

Stein, James D., 1941–
    The right decision : a mathematician reveals how the secrets of decision theory can help you make the right decision every time / James Stein.
        p.   cm.
    Includes index.
    ISBN: 978-0-07-161419-1 (alk. paper)
    1. Decision making.   I. Title.

    HD30.23.S72573   2010
    153.8′3—dc22   2009025460

1 2 3 4 5 6 7 8 9 10 11 12 13 14 15 16 17 18 19 20 21 22 23 24   FGR/FGR   0 9

ISBN   978-0-07-161419-1
MHID   0-07-161419-2

Interior design by Think Book Works

Contents

Preface

Making the Right Moves

I n a shaky economic time, should you hunker down and save money in the short term or do as the brilliant financier Bernard Baruch once advised and buy your straw hats in winter?

Should you try to make the best of a deteriorating relationship or cut your losses?

Should you stay in a comfortable job with little chance for advancement or take a risky one in which you could make lots of money or be out on the street?

One doctor advises surgery, but another thinks you should wait for a while and see if the situation improves. Which should you do?

Almost everyone will face at least one of these questions at least once, and many will face all of them. While you might escape with minimal damage if you make the wrong decision, it's not out of the realm of possibility that the wrong decision could wreck your life.

It would be nice to have a phalanx of experts to consult— a financial expert for the financial decisions, a medical advisor for health decisions, and an expert on personal relationships for decisions involving your interactions with others. Even nicer, however, would be the ability to stand on your own two feet and make such decisions accurately and with confidence. That's what this book proposes to help you do, by providing you with the principles of successful decision making as incorporated in a branch of mathematics known as *decision theory*. The principles of decision theory, derived from rigorous mathematical analysis, are widely used by major organizations in making strategic decisions, but they apply to all decisions—whether they involve your finances, your health, or your relationships.

You are what you decide—and there's a really good way to make those decisions.

It's Not Your Father's Mathematics

When you last looked at math, it was probably for stuff like finding areas of triangles and factoring polynomials—activities that now occupy 0 percent of your life. That's how math is generally used through high school, but if you go to college and major in science or engineering, you learn the mathematics of the eighteenth and nineteenth centuries. These branches of mathematics, originating in the work of Isaac Newton, prove incredibly successful in dealing with the physical universe and provide the basis for much of our technological civilization.

However, in the twentieth century, mathematics emerged from this cocoon and entered the world in which you and I live. Twentieth-century mathematics deals with politics, social interactions, psychology, economics, and business. A major mathematical development in this area—and one of which we will make extensive use—is *game theory*. Jointly developed by the mathematician John von Neumann and the economist Oskar Morgenstern, it has been applied to all of the subjects just mentioned. Decision theory is also a relatively recent arrival on the mathematical scene. It isn't necessary to understand mathematics to learn the principles of decision theory—for which I'm sure you're extremely grateful—and these principles can help anyone make better decisions.

No one would deny that it's an advantage to be born with a huge trust fund or incredible talent. But even if you are blessed with one or both, your life is basically the result of the decisions you make. Consistently making the right decisions is guaranteed to make your life improve because, by definition, the right decisions lead to a better quality of life. Making the right decisions is what this book is about.

Learning by Doing: How This Book Is Written

Nobody teaches a child to ride a bicycle by handing him or her a book, an instructional video, or an interactive bicycle-riding CD. You learn to ride a bicycle by getting on the bicycle and riding the bicycle. Of course, the parents initially work with a three-wheeler, then possibly training wheels, and then are very protective of the child as he or she goes through the initial stages of learning to ride a two-wheeler. But there is simply no substitute for the child actually getting on the bike.

And, in learning to make more effective decisions, there is simply no substitute for making decisions. So you'll be provided with the opportunity to make decisions—lots of decisions. That's the fun part of this book. There are basically three areas in life in which one can make decisions—decisions about personal relationships (such as what to do about that deteriorating relationship), decisions about what you should do with your life (whether to take a risky job, whether to have surgery), and decisions about the organizations, such as a business, in which you participate. You'll have lots of opportunities to practice all three kinds of decisions in this book—some examples we will discuss arise from common situations you may already have encountered. Many of the decisions you will encounter in this book are based on actual historical events. Some of these decisions changed the course of history, and some were critical in shaping the destinies of companies whose names are household words.

The principal character in this book is *you*—but there are also guest appearances by Albert Einstein, your parents, Microsoft, your spouse, JFK, your in-laws, Thomas Edison, your boss, IBM, your kids, Abraham Lincoln—and a host of other people and organizations whom you actually know or know of. They'll all play a part in helping you make better decisions.

The Learning Process

I was fortunate to have a wonderful teacher as a thesis advisor in graduate school. When I landed my first teaching job, I asked him for some advice. One of the things he said was that students always learn 30 percent of what you teach them, so teach them a lot.

I adopted this policy for five years or so and then came to a quite different conclusion. In any of the subjects I taught, there are a few core ideas, and everything else is an application or extension of them. As a result, my philosophy of teaching was to emphasize the few core ideas and hammer them home at every opportunity.

Other teachers have also reached this conclusion. Sometime in the mid-1990s, a friend I play tennis with went to Indian Wells to watch the major tournament that is held there every spring. At the time, Stefan Edberg, the world's number-one player, was coached by Tony Pickard, who had coached several other top players. Edberg was practicing on an outside court, and my friend moved in close so he could hear the words of wisdom that Pickard was imparting to Edberg.

What he heard was "Watch the ball." "Get your racket back early." "Move your feet." These are the first three things anyone who picks up a tennis racket is taught. No matter how good you are, these basic principles are critical to playing well—and Pickard was obviously aware of how important it was to reiterate them.

This book will give you a good grounding in the basic principles of decision theory. You'll be happy to learn that there aren't that many of them, and some will be familiar to you in specific environments. Once you start thinking of decisions in terms of general principles you can apply to the particulars of a specific decision, you will be well on your way to making better decisions—and to bettering your life.

Interactive Quizzes: The Core of This Book

I said earlier that the only way to really learn how to make good decisions is by making lots of decisions—and having them critiqued. A good coach tells you what you are doing right—and what you are doing wrong. He or she does that by watching you perform.

I can't watch you—but I can set up situations in which you have to make a decision, let you make it, and then critique the result. This is done by means of interactive quizzes. In each quiz, you'll be presented with a short description of a situation that calls for a decision and given three different alternatives to choose from. Make your choice and see how the alternatives are scored and read the rationale for that score.

The book is divided into two parts. The first part consists of a number of chapters that explain the basic ideas of decision theory, woven together with interactive quizzes so that you see how the principles apply. There's enough textual material for you to pick up the core ideas of decision theory but not enough to weigh you down. To continue with the analogy of learning to ride a bicycle, you certainly wouldn't give someone who's learning to ride a bike books on the history of the bicycle and the physics of riding it. You'd probably teach someone more quickly and successfully by arming them with the following basic concepts: "You've got to keep up a certain amount of speed, otherwise you won't be able to maintain your balance," and "If you start to turn the front wheel, there will be a tendency for the turn to continue and become a sharper turn." That's probably enough for starters.

Part 2, "The Quizzes," consists of interactive quizzes involving all the different aspects of decision theory. The quizzes in Part 2 are divided into four sets of seven quizzes each, so that you can do one a day at your convenience—you generally don't need more than five or ten minutes to complete each quiz. It takes much longer to do a crossword or sudoku puzzle, and when you do one of those a day for four weeks, your life won't have changed a whole lot. My hope is that you'll find these quizzes even more fun than crosswords or sudoku—and that, unlike crosswords and sudoku, they will change your life substantially for the better.

When you get to Part 2, you will note that all the quizzes appear on the right-hand page, with the solutions on the next left-hand page, so you do not get to see the solutions when you read the quizzes. I would have loved to have been able to do this throughout the entire book, but that would often have resulted in explanatory material that was either much too sparse or much too verbose. As a result, the solution to a quiz will sometimes start on the same page as a quiz or will appear on a facng page. It's up to you how you want to deal with this. You can either cover up the solutions to a greater or lesser extent, or allow yourself to take a peek. You might try one approach on one chapter and a different approach on another to see what works best for you.

Acknowledgments

I have been incredibly fortunate to have the assistance of three wonderful people on this book. Jodie Rhodes, my agent, may be the literary equivalent of James Brown—the hardest-working woman in the literary business. John Aherne, the editor, provided structure, guidance, and detailed criticism when necessary—and also had the courage to let me have free rein to write this book in my own somewhat quirky style. Finally, my wife, Linda, proofread the manuscript with the same exquisite care and attention to detail that she shows in running our household—helping me organize my life.

My thanks and appreciation to all three but especially to Linda.

PART 1

The Basics of Decision Theory

CHAPTER 1 # You Are What You Decide

S everal years ago, *Blink*, a very entertaining and thought-provoking book, appeared on the market. In it, Malcolm Gladwell analyzes the snap decision—how we are capable of assessing information very quickly (in the blink of an eye, hence the title) and often reaching the correct conclusion.

Gladwell was honest enough to include instances of such decisions leading to erroneous conclusions as well. However, I suspect that a large part of the appeal of the book was inherent in the subtitle: *The Power of Thinking Without Thinking*. Thinking is hard work, and most people simply don't want to do it. I've taught mathematics for more than forty years, and I am still amazed at the number of students who are willing to put in hours every day improving their bodies but regard the process of spending an hour a day studying math as inhuman punishment.

You are most definitely what you decide. Some decisions are, understandably, "blink" decisions; if you go to the zoo and all of a sudden a tiger breaks loose from the enclosure, run like hell. If, one enchanted evening, you should see a stranger across a crowded room and the two of you make lingering eye contact, negotiate your way across that crowded room and introduce yourself. However, if you are confronted with a life-altering decision, such as whether or not to have surgery, don't "blink." This is probably a really good time for analysis—real mathematical analysis that will lead you to the best decision.

This book will give you the tools to make good decisions. Life can be viewed as a game, and the decisions you make determine to a large extent whether you will be a winner or a loser. Life's winners, more often than not, are the product of good decisions, and life's losers are frequently the result of bad decisions. The purpose of this book is to help you make more good decisions and fewer bad ones—no matter what the situation.

The Stages of a Decision

Suppose that, all of a sudden, you're hungry for Chinese, so you go over to your neighborhood Chinese restaurant, peruse the menu, and opt for the hot and sour soup and moo shu pork. You've just gone through the three major stages of a decision. Circumstances have arisen that necessitate the making of a decision (you're hungry for Chinese), you lay out a bunch of alternatives (read the menu), and choose among the alternatives (place your order). Admittedly, the decision you just made is closer to being a "blink" decision than a rational one, although you may have given some thought to the constraints imposed by calories, cost, and cholesterol. Nonetheless, the majority of decisions are similar to this one in that circumstances necessitate that a choice is made among alternatives.

In general, the events of your life conspire to require the making of a decision, so you can't do much about the first stage.

When you're hungry for Chinese, you're hungry for Chinese. Depending upon the decision, you can exercise some influence over the alternatives and even propose creative ones. For instance, many Chinese restaurants have a page with entrées written in Chinese; you might take it upon yourself to ask your server exactly what these are (but beware of the sea cucumber). It is in the third stage, when you make your selection, that the rubber meets the road. This is where most of decision theory is concentrated.

To get a feel for the structure of the quizzes, here's your first opportunity to make a decision. It would be a good idea to make this one correctly, for at one time the future of Western civilization depended upon it, and the fact that the decision was successful is one of the reasons that you're reading this book in English rather than in German.

Second-in-Command

The U.S. government has just handed you, General Leslie Groves, the biggest blank check in history and with it a mission: to build the first atomic bomb. You're going to have to find a physicist to be your second-in-command because only physicists can build an atomic bomb (if it can be built at all), and a general is about as popular with physicists as a fox at a chicken convention. However, you've finally narrowed your choice to three possibilities, and you've even pinned nicknames on them:

A. Slim: a chain smoker who could charm the birds out of the trees. Everybody in the physics community loves him, but can you trust him? The FBI thinks he might have Communist affiliations.

B. **Sarge:** a monomaniacal anti-Nazi who could probably lead a platoon of raw recruits to take an enemy machine-gun nest. An émigré from Hungary, even those who dislike him admire him.

C. **Doc:** winner of a Nobel Prize, he may be the brightest of the lot. A brilliant theorist and technician, he has only recently arrived from Italy, and he's something of an unknown.

Nobody wants to think about the horrifying possibility that the Germans will get there first, so it is quite possible that Western civilization could be riding on your decision. Should you choose

A. Slim?
B. Sarge?
C. Doc?

SOLUTIONS: *Second-in-Command*

A. **Slim. 5 points.** Every decision has a goal, and often this goal can be quantified, that is, expressed in terms of numbers. *Quantifying results is an important part of making good decisions; these quantified results are called* payoffs, *and many decisions come down to how to maximize favorable payoffs or minimize adverse ones.* Your payoffs for this decision are measured in the number of top physicists you can motivate to work on the project. In order to get that done, they'll need to love both what they are doing and the man who makes them do it, and Slim is beloved in the physics community. Yes, you are a little worried about his purported Communist affiliations, but Communist countries are not the enemy in this conflict. Your money should be riding on Slim, who is much better known as J. Robert Oppenheimer.

B. **Sarge. 3 points.** A close runner-up. This guy obviously has leadership potential, and there are certainly situations in which the success of a mission may even be enhanced if some of the men on the line dislike the leader. Many military objectives have been captured by men who hate their sergeant so much that they just want to show up that SOB. If something happens to Oppenheimer, it might well be a good idea to go with Sarge, otherwise known as Edward Teller, later to be known as the father of the hydrogen bomb.

C. **Doc. 0 points.** This choice may well be counterproductive. Sometimes it is not a good idea to have the most talented individual be the administrative head, as you could be taking him away from doing what he does best. Because he is so brilliant, however, it is probably a good idea to make him the head of an important technical subproject. Doc, also known as Enrico Fermi, was actually placed in charge of developing a sustainable chain reaction, which he accomplished under the football stadium at the University of Chicago in December 1942.

WHAT ACTUALLY HAPPENED

In the fall of 1939, shortly after Adolf Hitler invaded Russia, a letter from Albert Einstein and Leo Szilard was delivered to President Franklin Roosevelt outlining the possibility of developing an atomic bomb. A committee to study the feasibility of such a weapon was formed; over the course of the next couple of years, it evolved into the Manhattan Project, headed by General Leslie Groves.

Against the advice of almost everyone, Groves took the risky step of placing J. Robert Oppenheimer in charge of Los Alamos National Laboratory, where the bomb was eventually built. Although Groves and Oppenheimer were almost complete opposites—Groves a methodical conservative, Oppenheimer a leftist intellectual—they were an extremely effective duo, and Groves's decision to appoint Oppenheimer was instrumental to the eventual success of the project.

Groves Probably Didn't "Blink"

Biographies of General Groves generally describe a conservative, methodical, and thoughtful individual. Oppenheimer was the exact opposite, a flashy leftist intellectual, and my guess is that had Groves made a "blink" decision, he would have gone with Edward Teller, whose values seemed to be much closer to those of Groves. (After the war, Teller was the force behind the development of the hydrogen bomb, which Oppenheimer opposed.) Teller, however, was not nearly as popular as Oppenheimer in the physics community, and had Groves appointed Teller, the Manhattan Project might not have attracted as many physicists, which would have reduced the chances of its success.

What You Can Learn from History: The Payoff Factor

The key to many successful decisions is to recognize that there is one *quantifiable factor* that is of paramount importance and that the decision succeeds or fails based on maximizing the payoffs associated with that factor. Problems making the correct decision in such a situation—when one factor outweighs all others—generally arise in two different ways. First and most obvious, other factors may cause the decision maker to take his or her eye off the ball. In the Manhattan Project scenario, had Groves been a rabid anti-Communist or had those above him in the chain of command been rabid anti-Communists, the decision to choose Oppenheimer would not have been so straightforward, and these secondary factors (the hypothetical anti-Communist sentiments of one of the contenders) might have eclipsed the *payoff* factor.

Additionally, it is sometimes not so easy to assess the payoffs of a given situation with a degree of certainty. This frequently happens in the real world, where markets for goods or services are often greatly underestimated or overestimated. Hollywood frequently invests millions of dollars in a movie with top stars only to have the movie flop completely because the payoff factor associated with its production—the number of viewers—was badly misjudged.

We frequently read of the successful businessperson who has abandoned the rat race for a simpler, although less financially rewarding, life. These decisions are payoff-motivated; the individual has simply decided that the most rewarding payoff structure for him or her is not a monetary one. Decisions that may seem inexplicable sometimes result from the choice of a payoff system—the units in which the payoffs are measured—that is very different from the one used by the observer to whom the decision seems inexplicable. Payoffs are simply numbers on a numerical scale, and once the units associated with these numbers—physicists, dollars, whatever—are determined, many decisions become clear-cut.

Decision Theory: An Unconventional Form of Mathematics

Learning decision theory is learning mathematics—but it isn't mathematics in the conventional sense of solving equations or finding the areas of triangles. Decision theory is mathematics in the sense that it encompasses basic principles and concepts, such as payoffs, principles relating to those basic concepts, and a wide range of applicability of those concepts.

Decision theory, though, is unlike much of mathematics in that many of its core principles can be expressed using language that is familiar and easy to understand. When Tony Pickard told Stefan Edberg to watch the ball, he wasn't just uttering an injunction so common it had become a cliché, he was reminding Edberg that watching the ball is a critical component of the production of a good shot. Watching the ball is key in practically any game that uses a ball, such as baseball, football, or golf.

"Focus on the payoff factor" is the "watch the ball" of decision theory. Payoffs are how the success of the decision is scored. The payoffs in some decisions are money, in others, contentment or happiness, and in still others, physicists. Not every decision involves payoffs, but a great many do, and failure to recognize the underlying payoff scheme in a decision is the equivalent of taking your eye off the ball.

By the Numbers

Much of mathematics works with quantities or collections of quantities—and many of the concepts of decision theory can be visualized through the use of numerical examples, which will appear in this and subsequent "By the Numbers" sections. As the concepts become more sophisticated, the numerical examples will mirror this.

For instance, suppose that General Groves could have come up with really good numerical estimates for the number of physicists each possible choice would attract and assemble them in a row as follows:

	OPPENHEIMER	TELLER	FERMI
Number of Physicists	200	120	80

Mathematicians would call the row of three numbers presented here a *payoff vector.* If there is only one possible payoff vector in a problem, all we have to do is choose the alternative with the most attractive payoff number. (As we shall see, there are times you want to choose the alternative with the smallest payoff number rather than the largest.)

There, that wasn't so bad, was it?

Rationality and Pragmatism

A final note before delving further into decision theory. Decision theory evaluates decisions according to a number of rational criteria. In other words, there are logical reasons that a particular decision should be made. General Groves chose Oppenheimer for the Manhattan Project because he wanted as many physicists as possible to willingly work on the project; the greater the number of physicists, the greater the chances for success. From a pragmatic point of view, this was the winning decision, as the Manhattan Project was ultimately successful.

Unfortunately, the correct decision (from the standpoint of rationality) is not always the successful decision. Other than looking into the future, there is no way of ensuring a successful decision—so be wary of any book, person, or website that claims to give an ironclad guarantee. It is certainly possible that a cadre of physicists who did not decide to work on the Manhattan Project because Oppenheimer was in charge might have done so had Teller been appointed. Indeed, one can envision circumstances in which an Oppenheimer-directed Manhattan Project might have failed, whereas a Teller-directed one would have succeeded. However, Groves made what sports fans would call "the percentage play," the decision that was more likely to be successful. Choosing an alternative with the greatest probability of success is one rational criterion—but not the only one, and sometimes not the correct one—in the context of a particular decision.

CHAPTER 2 # Creating the Menu

Once you recognize that you need to make a decision, you find yourself in the second stage of the decision process, setting out the alternatives confronting you. This is an extremely important stage, one that many people tend to overlook. Far too often, decisions are made by accepting the first reasonable alternative—or even worse, simply the first alternative—that occurs to the person making the decision.

Decision theory is a collection of tools for structuring and choosing among a finite number of qualitatively different alternatives. For instance, if you go into the supermarket intent upon ordering some ground hamburger, you are in theory confronted with innumerable possible alternatives—from a quarter of a pound all the way up to whatever quantity of hamburger the store has on hand. Deciding how much hamburger to buy, which is simply choosing an appropriate value of a single parameter, such as weight, is generally a matter of economic considerations, such as whether the hamburger is on sale, and how much storage room is available in the freezer compartment of your refrigerator.

This is not a choice likely to be aided by decision theory. Deciding how to use the hamburger in tonight's menu can be a problem to which decision theory is applicable—if you are only able to prepare one dish, should you make your crowd-pleasing meat loaf, which everyone loves but which requires a lot of work, or simply prepare hamburgers, which take substantially less effort but generally garner less than rave reviews?

Decision theory also deals only with alternatives that can actually be selected. If a young male decides that he is going to date Angelina Jolie, that is probably not under his control, is not a reasonable alternative, and is therefore not well served by decision theory.

In creating a menu of alternatives, it is wise to set some limit on the number of possibilities. For example, when purchasing a bottle of wine, a reasonable strategy is to decide what type of wine to buy (say, Merlot or Pinot Noir) and approximately what one is willing to pay, then selecting from the alternatives that fall into the selected category. If you decided to buy a bottle of wine by checking out every bottle in the store, you'd invest all day in something that should probably only require a few minutes. For all the decision quizzes presented in this book, the reader is provided a choice of only three possible alternatives; three is a tractable number of options to consider.

One reason that many important decisions generally have three alternatives is because there is often a factor central to the decision that has two extreme positions and one moderate one. Investment often falls into this category—one can invest very conservatively or very aggressively, or construct a portfolio that achieves a middle ground. Political issues often feature three basic approaches—liberal, conservative, and middle-of-the-road. Let's examine one such decision that changed America.

Position Paper

Your conscience tells you that slavery must be abolished, but on the other hand, you—Abraham Lincoln—are in the middle of a civil war that could go either way. The radical faction of the Republican Party is pressing you, as president, to abolish slavery, while the conservative faction is substantially more cautious. These aren't the only problems you have to contend with. As it is up to you to hold what remains of the Union together, you can't afford to upset too many people. In particular, you've got to be extremely careful, in formulating a policy, not to upset the border states, which do not have the ferocious antislavery attitude that characterizes some of the more northern states. There's a lot of push and shove going on, and you're going to have to make some sort of announcement on this complex issue. Considering that you have both your conscience and the Union to account to, should you

A. **decide that, sooner or later, the bullet is going to have to be bitten and come out with an emancipation proclamation that completely abolishes slavery now?**

B. **announce that, while you personally are against slavery, since times are difficult and the position complex, you are indefinitely postponing a decision on what action to take?**

C. **take a halfway position and abolish slavery at some fixed date in the future while specifically exempting the border states?**

SOLUTIONS: *Position Paper*

A. **You decide that, sooner or later, the bullet is going to have to be bitten and come out with an emancipation proclamation that completely abolishes slavery now. 1 point.** This decision turns on what attitude you are going to take regarding slavery. The difficulty with selecting this alternative is that it runs the risk of alienating some very important political factions at an extremely delicate moment in the war. This is one of the extreme positions on the what-do-do-about-slavery spectrum, and as pointed out in the previous sentence, there is a huge negative associated with this alternative.

B. **You announce that, while you personally are against slavery, since times are difficult and the position complex, you are indefinitely postponing a decision on what action to take. 0 points.** This is the other extreme alternative that you can reasonably ponder, as a proslavery stance was simply not an option that Lincoln could consider. There are often times when delay is advisable, in particular when delay will enable information to be gained that will make possible a more accurate decision. This, however, is not such a case. Taking a clear-cut position now will generate both support and opposition, but delaying an announcement of your choice will be viewed as indecision. When you finally take a position, even those who agree with that position may wonder about the strength of your commitment.

C. **You take a halfway position and abolish slavery at some fixed date in the future while specifically exempting the border states. 5 points.** Whenever extreme actions are judged to yield unsatisfactory results, compromise actions must be considered. *While no compromise will satisfy all parties, the increase in payoffs from those who agree with the compromise may well more than compensate for the decrease in payoffs from those who disagree with it.*

WHAT ACTUALLY HAPPENED

Most people are under the impression that Lincoln selected action A and completely abolished slavery immediately. His actual choice was the compromise, action C, and was obviously the winning decision. Lincoln, later known as the Great Emancipator, was not just an idealist—he was a realist who knew the importance of the role of compromise in making winning decisions.

What You Can Learn from History

You can't make a winning decision if the winning alternative is not on the table. Lincoln's decision illustrates two extremely important ideas. First, try to figure out what the extreme alternatives of the decision are. "Extremes" are often defined in terms of such opposites as "safe or risky," "liberal or conservative," etc. Not all decisions feature such opposites as an integral part of the decision, but many do. Second, spend some time looking for possible compromise alternatives. They do not always readily suggest themselves, but finding them sometimes generates the "eureka" moment of having found the best solution. Compromises must be judged on whether the payoff increase from those who like the compromise offsets the payoff decrease from those who don't.

Parametric and Nonparametric Decisions

Some decisions, such as "how safe or how risky" or "how liberal or how conservative," can be placed on a single scale where the decision is defined by the quantity of a single parameter, such as risk or conservatism. In the Lincoln example, selecting alternatives involved defining the extreme positions and then searching for the middle ground. Many everyday situations involve choices for which there is no convenient parameter or scale by which we can measure the choices. Mom's question "What would you like for dinner?" might be met by Dad's preference for meat loaf, Junior's for spaghetti, and Sis's for salad. While one could measure the choices in terms of a parameter like calories or grams of carbohydrates, neither of these parameters is likely to figure significantly into Mom's decision.

To Your Good Health

The recent elections have brought health care to the forefront of the national agenda, and you're all smiles. You wouldn't mind seeing the First Amendment to the Constitution updated to include the right to health care because that's your business. You're the head of a chain of hospitals that form a regional health maintenance organization (HMO), and expansion is definitely in the cards. You're planning on moving both upward and outward, increasing the range of coverage you provide and moving outside your geographic region. What you need now are some analysts to help you figure out what to do. Should you concentrate your resources on hiring

A. **legislative analysts, who can tell you which area of the country will provide a business climate that is friendliest to the type of organization you intend to create?**
B. **demographic analysts, who will provide an overview of the types of services that will most likely be required?**
C. **cost analysts, who will be able to project the price of the pharmaceuticals and services you will need to supply?**

SOLUTIONS: *To Your Good Health*

A. **You hire legislative analysts, who can tell you which area of the country will provide a business climate that is friendliest to the type of organization you intend to create. 5 points.** All the other aspects of your business change relatively slowly. True, a new surgical technique or new drug can have a decided impact on a small percentage of your business, but a legislature that is either friendly or hostile to your industry can determine whether you prosper, survive, or fail. Since the rules governing your industry vary from state to state, make sure you set up shop where conditions are most favorable. *When alternatives cannot be directly compared by looking at payoffs, as is generally the case in nonparametric decisions such as this one, it can often be helpful to look at which factors most crucially impact the success or failure of the decision.*

B. **You hire demographic analysts, who will provide an overview of the types of services that will most likely be required. −1 point.** Yes, if you go to Florida, you'll have a lot of retirees, but you don't really need experts to point this out. You can probably find a publicly available population database to research this fairly quickly, and you don't need experts to help you. Money spent here is basically money out the window.

C. **You hire cost analysts, who will be able to project the price of the pharmaceuticals and services you will need to supply. 1 point.** This would definitely be helpful to your bottom line, but it's not clear how accurate such projections will be. You are looking to see into the future here, and if you want to hire prognosticators, hire prognosticators with expertise in the area which will most critically affect your financial picture.

Asking the Right Questions

Every teacher has a philosophy of education, and one of the advantages of teaching at a college is that your classroom is your fiefdom, where you can impose your philosophy of education by fiat. Although I believe that finding answers is more important than asking questions, unless one acquires the ability to ask *the right* questions *that directly pertain to the problem at hand*, asking a bunch of questions doesn't really accomplish anything. Many classes in mathematics have both lecture sessions and activity sessions; the teacher presents the material in the lecture sessions and uses the activity sessions to enhance the learning experience. I use activity sessions to answer any questions the students have—most of the time I simply do homework problems by request, but occasionally students ask questions about relevance or applicability. I don't judge the relative value of their questions; I simply answer them. An important part of education, as opposed to simply the assimilation of knowledge and techniques in a particular area, is the ability to ask questions that have helpful answers. In the previous quiz, the right question is "What factor has the most effect on the profitability of the business?"

Actions and the Butterfly Effect

One of the more intriguing discoveries of mid-twentieth-century mathematics is the "butterfly effect." Some systems are so sensitive to certain parameters that small changes in those parameters can result in significant changes to the system. The classic example, for which the butterfly effect was named, is that the global weather system is so sensitive to certain variations that, theoretically, whether or not a butterfly flaps its wings in Hawaii can determine whether a tornado occurs in Oklahoma several weeks later.

Decision theory has its own version of the butterfly effect, as illustrated in the previous quiz. The attitudes of the two political parties, Republicans and Democrats, are generally considerably different on many of the major issues, such as health care. It is easy to envision that the election of a single Republican (or Democrat) could alter the balance of power in a legislative body, significantly impacting the legislation that it passes. This is the butterfly effect in action and highlights that the composition of a legislative body is of extreme importance in determining the future of many businesses. As a result, a great deal of money is spent hiring both legislative analysts and lobbyists—like you didn't know that, but you may not have realized that this is an example of a decision-making principle that can be used in other areas. Fortunately, you can often tell what decisions may have a major impact on your life. Failing to practice your putting prior to your Saturday golf game is far less likely to matter in the long run than failing to bone up on the workings of a company with whom you have an upcoming job interview. Concentrate on what really matters.

Let's take a look at another real-world decision.

A Row of Ducks

As the final quarter of the nineteenth century approaches, you, Thomas Edison, foresee a coming era of greater and greater use of machines, particularly those that use electricity. As a result, you are planning on going into business developing those machines. Not only are you very talented, but you have always been able to keep your eye on the ball—when you were young, you saved the life of a railway station official's child and asked for lessons in telegraphy as a reward. Despite the fact that you have little or no formal schooling, you have already developed several improvements to the telegraph, and this has given you a modest amount of seed money. As a result, you are nearly at the point where you can start your own company developing inventions. You already have several inventions in mind, but in order for your business to become prosperous, you want to make sure that all your ducks are in a row. The two inventions that you believe have top priority are a stock quotations printer and an electric light. Should you

A. develop the stock quotations printer first, as there is an immediate demand for it, although the market is small?

B. develop the electric light first because the market for it is so phenomenally large that it is certain to make you rich once electricity is widely available?

C. share work on both projects initially and then concentrate your efforts on whichever project is coming along best?

SOLUTIONS: *A Row of Ducks*

A. **You develop the stock quotations printer first, as there is an immediate demand for it, although the market is small. 5 points.** The first order of business is to stay in business. To do that, you need money. This may not make you a fortune, but it's quick money. Remember the injunction to concentrate on what really matters? Staying in business is what really matters.

B. **You develop the electric light first because the market for it is so phenomenally large that it is certain to make you rich once electricity is widely available. 3 points.** This would not be the worst mistake ever made, considering that you will probably make the most money once this is successful. If your financial position were more secure, you could afford to put your time and energy into making the most money from a single invention.

C. **You share work on both projects initially and then concentrate your efforts on whichever project is coming along best. 1 point.** It is important that you realize that by choosing this action you may run out of money before you have a marketable product because the arithmetic of inventions is that two half-inventions do not make a whole. Additionally, you can only ride out the period before the electric light becomes profitable if you have sufficient funds, and the only place to obtain them is from the stock quotations printer. Therefore, the printer must have priority.

WHAT ACTUALLY HAPPENED

Edison initially developed the stock quotations printer and used this money, and money from his telegraphic inventions, to start the world's first major research-and-development center. Edison always made sure that a market existed before starting work on a project, which is an approach rooted in decision theory—know your payoffs, and use relevant decision criteria.

It's also interesting that when Edison tackled the lightbulb project, he examined thousands of different materials before finding the right one to use as the filament. He could afford the time spent on this because he had lined up his ducks by developing the stock quotations printer first and had the time and money needed for the lightbulb project.

What You Can Learn from History

The arithmetic of projects is very similar to the arithmetic of inventions. One nearly finished project plus one half-finished project plus one project in development equals no completed projects. The world is littered with half-finished products, half-written screenplays (especially in Hollywood)—and half-baked ideas. To paraphrase a remark made by Dustin Hoffmann in *The Graduate*, you've got to make sure that your projects are fully baked.

Many projects require a critical mass of ideas in order to explode in fully developed glory. Think of all the storefronts you've seen empty because the tenants ran out of money before the store could become operational. When you have only a limited supply of gunpowder, heed the words given to the American soldiers at the battle of Bunker Hill—don't fire 'til you see the whites of their eyes. Make sure you can complete whatever decision you make.

CHAPTER 3 What's in It for Me?

Determining Your Payoffs

Who you become depends to a great extent on what you decide—but who you are and what you value frequently determine what the best decision is.

In the first chapter we encountered the idea of payoffs—a numerical scale by which the alternatives for many decisions can be evaluated. The payoff system, the units in which the payoffs are evaluated, that was adopted by General Leslie Groves was the number of top physicists that could be attracted to working on the Manhattan Project. However, frequently there are payoff systems involving different units in play. Almost all parents play games with their children involving both physical and mental activities. It is the rare parent who has a young child who is so talented that the child can win on the basis of ability alone. Although chess prodigies do appear at incredibly young ages, they are extremely rare—but the number of parents who have lost games of chess or Scrabble or H-O-R-S-E to their children is doubtless in the hundreds of millions. These parents have deliberately lost games to their children because they judge that their payoffs are not measured by victory but by other factors such as the pleasure and possible growth of their children.

The diversity of payoffs has ramifications in decision theory. Decisions are not generally right or wrong according to some abstract set of principles but are right or wrong in the context of the values of the person making the decision. Had General Groves been an enemy agent rather than a patriotic American, his goal would have been to minimize, rather than maximize, the number of physicists working on the Manhattan Project. This would have

By the Numbers

The decisions discussed in this section center around the selection of an appropriate payoff vector. Instead of being confronted with a single payoff vector, as was General Groves in the Manhattan Project scenario, imagine that we have two payoff vectors as in the following example.

	ALTERNATIVE A	ALTERNATIVE B	ALTERNATIVE C
Vector 1	10	7	3
Vector 2	3	6	8

The dilemma here isn't selecting the correct alternative, it's selecting the correct vector—but different individuals might make different choices because they have different values. In the previous example, the first vector might refer to the financial payoffs associated with three different job opportunities, while the second vector might refer to the overall desirability of the cities in which the jobs are located. What's sauce for the goose need not be sauce for the gander.

resulted in the selection of someone other than Oppenheimer—because the payoffs would have been measured in the number of physicists dissuaded from working on the project.

There is an old saying to the effect that you should be very careful what you wish for—for you might get it. The same is true of making decisions. Make sure you understand what you really want—that if you achieve the payoffs for which you are striving, the end result will be what you want. Many decisions fail because they maximize the wrong payoffs—a point realized too late by the men who achieve financial success at the cost of an unhappy marriage.

The Mentor

Ever since that unforgettable Christmas when your parents gave you a microscope, you've dreamed of being a biologist. You could have gone into industry or taught biology at a high school after you received your B.S., but you had your sights set on getting a doctorate. You had to take out a bunch of student loans, and undoubtedly a major factor in the recent rise in fuel prices is all the midnight oil you've had to burn. However, it all seems to have paid off—at least at this stage. You've just gotten word that you've passed your comprehensive exams, and it's time to select a thesis advisor. You've heard the horror stories about promising students who have been derailed by selecting the wrong advisor, so this is obviously a make-or-break decision. Should you choose

A. **the department curmudgeon?** Nobody really likes him, but he has a very good track record of turning out Ph.D.s, even if—as it is rumored—they have to mow his lawn as part of the deal.

B. **the hotshot?** Two years ago he produced a thesis that has the largest number of citations of any publication produced by a member of the department. There's a chance that he's doing research that will put him on the short list for a Nobel Prize.

C. **your favorite professor?** You instantly connected with this guy, you know you can work with him, and he's willing to let you choose whatever topic you would like for your dissertation.

SOLUTIONS: *The Mentor*

A. **The department curmudgeon. 5 points.** You've got to keep your eye on the ball here *as payoffs are the means by which you evaluate the relative merits of many decisions.* Your payoffs are determined by the likelihood that you will end up with a doctorate, and this guy is a proven producer. You don't have to like him, you may have to get in shape to mow his lawn, but you haven't run this particular race to fail to make it over the final hurdle.

B. **The hotshot. −1 point.** There are two major strikes against him. First of all, he's inexperienced—he might easily select a problem for you to tackle that is simply too difficult or takes too long to get results. Second, if really good things happen, he's likely to get the credit, not you. Comparing him with the department curmudgeon is like selecting a surgeon. You don't want a guy who'll make the medical journals but one who'll get you through the operation successfully.

C. **Your favorite professor. 3 points.** There are pros and cons here. If you *know* with total certainty that you have a topic that will result in a dissertation, this is definitely the guy to choose. You'll enjoy the experience, and you'll get the credit. However, his attitude may be a little too laissez-faire; he's letting you make decisions that he should probably make. While there is no way that choosing the hotshot can work, things could work out gloriously here— but possibly not. The more confident you are in your own abilities, the more you should go with this guy.

What Really Counts

We live in a world in which style is often favored over substance— and we're not the first generation to experience this, nor will we be the last. Remember, when Lincoln was confronted with evidence of General Ulysses Grant's fondness for whiskey, he focused not on presumed character defects but on battlefield results—the bottom line for a wartime general. It's results, aka payoffs, that count in a lot of areas. I'd rather have an internist that I can discuss my health comfortably with than a cold fish, but when I go in for surgery I don't want personality, I want demonstrated ability.

Hacking It

Although you may hate to admit it, most people probably think of you as a computer geek. Well, you could be a lot worse; you're a look-alike, and possibly an act-alike, for Bill Gates, CEO of Microsoft, and his net worth is somewhere in the gazillions. If you had been born a century ago, you might have lived out your life as an underpaid clerk in a dreary desk job with some company, but as the twenty-first century moves into its second decade, you are eagerly looking forward to doing what you do best: sitting in a room, just you and the computer, and happily working away at programming puzzles both perplexing and profitable. Sometime in the hopefully not-too-distant future you intend to be an independent contractor; that way you can work out of your apartment and live life at your own pace in your own space. Meanwhile, however, you are going to take a job in the software industry, but you want to take one that will bring that not-too-distant future measurably closer. Should you work for

A. a scientific programming firm, which features the most interesting and intellectually challenging jobs?

B. an actuarial firm, which is currently short of programming talent and has offered the most attractive salary with an attractive sign-on bonus to boot?

C. a service bureau, which will send you out on a variety of jobs, possibly ranging from the sublime to the ridiculous?

SOLUTIONS: *Hacking It*

A. You take a job with a scientific programming firm, which features the most interesting and intellectually challenging jobs. 3 points. How are you going to measure your payoffs? If you are measuring them in terms of job interest or friends made, this is probably the best bet.

B. You sign on with an actuarial firm, which is currently short of programming talent and has offered the most attractive salary with an attractive sign-on bonus to boot. 1 point. Whenever money can be chosen as a possible unit for payoffs, there is a tendency to do so. If you wanted a condo and a BMW now, this would be the most attractive action, but your long-term goal is to be an independent contractor. *Don't get distracted by high payoffs if they're in the wrong units.*

C. **You work for a service bureau, which will send you out on a variety of jobs, possibly ranging from the sublime to the ridiculous. 5 points.** Your payoffs for this decision are measured not in friends, not in money, but in potential *contacts* who may contract with you in the future, enabling you to live the life that you want. Once you realize what you want in the way of payoffs here, the choice is obvious.

Knowing who you are and what you want are critical factors in making the right decision. These are clearly factors that are intertwined. Sometimes who you are is precisely who you want to be, as in the preceding quiz, but sometimes who you want to be is not who you are, and this fact determines what you want.

Decision theory deals with making the best possible choice in certain situations—but the best possible choice frequently depends critically on the payoff scheme. The payoff scheme, in turn, is selected by the individual making the decision. This book includes a wide variety of quizzes involving people with a variety of different payoff systems—from the noble to the reprehensible. Obviously, it would be preferable if better decisions were made by people with noble payoff schemes, but the purpose of the book is to enable *you* to make better decisions. By placing you in different situations involving people whose payoffs differ considerably from yours, you will become more versed in the principles that result in successful decisions.

History is replete with people who have faced critical decisions that involved knowing who they are and what they want, as in the following situation.

Green Thumb

You were so frail and sickly as a child that nobody ever thought you'd grow, but not only did you grow, everything you touched did as well. Yours was the classic tale of a child who wanted an education so badly that he sacrificed everything to obtain it. Your excellent high school record got you accepted as a scholarship student, but when you were instructed to report in September 1886, the fact that you were black prevented you from gaining admission, a humiliating experience that you would remember all your life. Eventually, though, you realized your goal of achieving a college degree when you majored in botany and agricultural chemistry at Iowa State. Finally, your talents were recognized when Iowa State appointed you to the faculty while you were working for your master's degree. It seems that when opportunity knocks, it practically pounds down your door. You are happy at Iowa State, and they are offering you a better position, but an agricultural firm is bidding for your services by offering a higher salary. In addition, the legendary black leader Booker T. Washington would like you to move to Tuskegee, Alabama, to take over his newly formed Normal and Industrial Institute for Negroes. Well, George Washington Carver, should you

A. **continue teaching at Iowa State, as you are clearly happy there?**

B. **take the job with the agricultural firm, which offers a higher salary?**
C. **move to Alabama to assist Booker T. Washington?**

SOLUTIONS: *Green Thumb*

A. **You continue teaching at Iowa State, as you are clearly happy there. 3 points.** Sometimes payoffs are externally determined, and in other instances, they are determined by one's values. In this case, your lifelong love of learning ranks very high on your scale of values, and because you are happy here, there is obviously strong incentive to continue with a winning action.

B. **You take the job with the agricultural firm, which offers a higher salary. −1 point.** Nothing in your life would lead you to believe that your payoffs are financially determined. If they were to offer you a million dollars, you would certainly consider it because it would enable you to pursue worthwhile goals, but a competitive offer would simply not supply worthwhile payoffs. *Unless the payoffs in a less attractive value system are off the scale, it is usually a mistake to jump at what appears to be a superficially tempting alternative that requires you to abandon your primary values.*

C. **You move to Alabama to assist Booker T. Washington. 5 points.** Here is an opportunity to both have your cake and eat it, too. Your values are not only related to education, they are also related to the experiences you have suffered as a black man in a world in which blacks find an education extraordinarily difficult to obtain. This action clearly maximizes your payoffs, and you should jump at the opportunity.

WHAT ACTUALLY HAPPENED

Carver immediately wrote Washington that he would take the job and thus began the career of one of America's greatest scientists. Carver almost single-handedly caused a massive increase in the agricultural prosperity of the South by developing numerous products that could be made from peanuts and soybeans, which helped convince farmers to diversify their crops.

What You Can Learn from History

There is one system of payoffs that trumps most of the others—happiness. In case of a conflict between differing systems of payoffs, see if there is a way to evaluate which decision, if successful, will make you happiest.

The next situation to confront you is one that possibly confronted you in the past, or will confront you—or your children—in the not-too-distant future.

College Material

Your parents were on the last plane out of Vietnam, with only a few meager possessions and the hope of a new life. They succeeded beyond their wildest dreams, and as a result, you are in an excellent position to realize their dreams—and yours—by attending college and going on to law school after that. Your father worked two jobs to enable you to attend a small private school in the San Fernando Valley rather than the dismal public school in the neighborhood where they set up the first of their three grocery stores. Your 4.6 GPA and combined score of 2140 on the SATs attest to the fact that, while you may not be brilliant, you are certainly more than diligent. You'd hate to make a false step at this stage, so you want to choose your college very carefully. You—and your parents—have narrowed it down to the following three institutions, and they have left it to you to choose the one you prefer. Your choices are

A. **UCLA.** It's well known as the "University of California with Lots of Asians"—and lots of everybody else. It ranks only behind Berkeley in the U of C system.
B. **Whittier College.** A small liberal arts college located in the attractive town of Whittier, it not only has Richard Nixon as an alumnus but also—surprise!—a law school.
C. **Stanford.** Every student has a dream college, and this one was yours. Initially you were on the waiting list, but the second mailing came in a big, overstuffed envelope, and you know that not many law schools turn down Stanford graduates.

SOLUTIONS: *College Material*

A. **UCLA. 4 points.** This seems like an environment in which you can succeed—it's a good school, and it's so large that you're bound to find a major and classes that will be a good fit. The only negative is the size; you come from a small-school background and did well there, and you don't know how you will survive in a large herd.
B. **Whittier College. 5 points.** This school has everything going for it as far as you're concerned, and it's a big plus when there are no minuses. As mentioned, you do well in a small-school environment, and even though it's small, it's a quality school. Remember, Richard Nixon started out as

a lawyer. How many schools can claim a president of the United States as an alumnus?

C. Stanford. 1 point. Yes, it's Stanford, and it greases the wheels to a successful future. But is it right for you? There are two red flags here—your SAT scores are low for a top-rated institution, and you got in on the second round. That doesn't mean that you can't make it here, but it's somewhat risky. You—and your parents—have worked much too hard to roll the dice. *Sometimes the payoffs down the road are so attractive that they obscure the near-term difficulties in obtaining them. Present obstacles diminish future payoffs.*

Utility—Some Payoffs Are More Equal Than Others

The way that we value payoffs depends on what we want, what we need—and when we need it. A bottle of water could be the difference between life and death in the desert but costs only a few cents at a local supermarket. We do not value our dollars identically, either. If someone in your family needed an immediate operation for which an up-front payment of $10,000 were required, this $10,000 would be vastly more valuable to you than the $1,000,000 in the will that is bequeathed to you by your eccentric uncle, who is in good physical health and might well live for another few decades.

Future payoffs, like future money, must be discounted by taking into consideration the passage of time that will be necessary to achieve them. Unlike money, though, your payoff scheme may change in the future. Ten dollars promised to you a year from now will not buy as much goods that it would if you had the ten dollars now—but it will certainly buy a reasonable amount of goods. As the physicist Niels Bohr once remarked, "It is very difficult to make an accurate prediction—especially about the future." If you plan to invest some time in attaining payoffs, be sure that when you attain them, you will still want them. Be sure as well that the payoffs you achieve are the important ones for accomplishing your goals.

The common theme of the quizzes in this chapter is that it is up to you to know what your payoffs are. It may sound a little cynical, but decision theory answers the biblical question "What shall it profit a man if he gains the whole world and loses his soul?" by responding that it depends how you measure your payoffs.

CHAPTER 4

When the Crystal Ball Is Cloudy

There are basically two types of decisions—those for which you can be certain of the outcome when you select an alternative and those for which you can only estimate how relatively likely or unlikely an outcome is when you select an alternative. This is the point at which the mathematics of *probability theory* enters the picture. In fact, it is a key component of decision theory.

It isn't necessary to take a course in probability theory to assimilate some of the basics. You know most of what you need to know from your familiarity with the weather report. The probability of an event is an estimate of its likelihood of occurring on a scale of 0 percent (can't happen) to 100 percent (dead certain), although mathematicians use a scale from 0 to 1 for formal computations. Here's an example.

Incentive Program

As part of a campaign to boost sales, the company's top brass has established a competition with a first prize of a week's all-expense-paid vacation for two in Paris, and you have your heart set on winning it. With just a few days to go, you are firmly entrenched in second place, within striking distance of the leader, who is off on a fishing expedition for new accounts in the Midwest. You've been on similar scouting trips yourself, and you know from experience that you usually land a few accounts on these trips—rarely striking out but rarely hitting home runs, either. Your opponent, the current leader, is going to call the home office in the next day or two and will then learn what your plans are. Although you cannot control his results, it's up to you to take advantage of what you know in order to devise a strategy that will give you the best chance of winning that trip to Paris by simultaneously improving your own chances and reducing his. Should you

A. **pursue a high-risk account that would practically guarantee victory if you landed it but that you must admit you have little or no chance of getting?**

B. **lock up some renewals, which would give you a victory under the assumption that the current sales leader has an exceptionally unproductive midwestern trip?**

C. **pursue an account that you have a reasonable, but not great, shot at getting, which will give you the victory unless your chief rival has an exceptionally good week?**

SOLUTIONS: *Incentive Program*

A. You pursue a high-risk account that would practically guarantee victory if you landed it but that you must admit you have little or no chance of getting. 1 point. *You should generally be reluctant to commit to a low-probability chance of victory unless it really is desperation time.* While there are times when competitive situations call for desperate measures and you have to throw a "Hail Mary" pass on the last play of the game in order to have any chance, too often wild gambles are hazarded before they are actually required.

B. You lock up some renewals, which would give you a victory under the assumption that the current sales leader has an exceptionally unproductive midwestern trip. −1 point. It is imperative that you put some pressure on your opponent by forcing him to acknowledge that you have adopted a plan that contains some potential for victory. He is extremely unlikely to have an unproductive midwestern trip, *unless* you can make him realize that it might be important for him to have a productive one. Choosing this action essentially makes it impossible for you to win; the only good thing that can happen is that your opponent might lose, and this is unlikely. It's bad strategy not to give your opponent a chance to lose.

C. You pursue an account that you have a reasonable, but not great, shot at getting, which will give you the victory unless your chief rival has an exceptionally good week. 5 points. This may appear to be the winner by default, but it would still stand out even if you weren't comparing it to the others. Two events have to happen for you to win: you have to land this account, and your opponent must fail to have a fantastic week. Nothing your opponent can do can affect your chances to land this account, but by forcing him to realize that he may have to put in an outstanding performance, you may be decreasing the probability that he will do so. Few perform well under pressure.

Ideally, it would be nice to be able to attach an accurate number from 0 percent to 100 percent to the likelihood of a particular outcome, but it isn't necessary. If you simply assess outcomes as "likely," "maybe," and "unlikely," you'll generally get a good enough estimate in order to proceed intelligently. For example, in the quiz you just did, you can assess the probability of your landing a high-risk account as "unlikely," the probability of locking up some renewals as "likely," and so forth. However, the success of each option is determined by two factors: the probability that it will occur and the reward associated with it.

One thing that you have undoubtedly learned in life is that greater rewards are associated with greater risk. It is rare to encounter a situation in which one alternative has a greater risk and a lesser reward than another action, but if that is the case, it is clear that the action with greater risk and lesser reward should not even be considered.

Decisions in the face of uncertainty have played an important role in the shaping of today's world, and many decisions, had they been made differently, would have resulted in a world that looks considerably different from the one we inhabit. Here's a good example—and a good opportunity for you to test your decision-making skills.

The Family Jewels

It's nice to have wealth and power, and as queen of Spain, you've got both. As always, those two assets attract a long line of people seeking your support. The latest in the afore-mentioned long line of people seeking your support is an Italo-Spanish explorer named Christopher Columbus. He has this wild idea that the Earth is round and by sailing west from Spain, he can discover a short trade route to Asia. This venture could be extremely profitable, but (a) it's going to cost an arm and a leg, (b) there is certainly no guarantee that he is right, and (c) even if he is right, you can't be sure that he'll deliver the goods. He tried this proposal on the king of Portugal, who turned him down. He tried it on a Spanish commission—same result. Now he's hitting on you. Should you

A. **turn him down, realizing that the odds are long and nobody else feels that he has a reasonable shot?**
B. **finance his fleet of three ships, realizing that you're going to have to sell the family jewels to do so?**
C. **give him partial support by supplying him with enough funds for one ship to get him started?**

SOLUTIONS: *The Family Jewels*

A. **You turn him down, realizing that the odds are long and nobody else feels that he has a reasonable shot. 5 points.** The man has a good story, but the combination of the probability that he is right *and* that he can accomplish his goal makes this proposition a substantial underdog. *The probability of two events* both *happening is* *generally significantly less than the probability of a single event happening.* Even if he succeeds, his success will not guarantee you substantial payoffs in the form of profits from increased trade with Asia. The king of Portugal and the Spanish commission who already turned him down are no fools, and you can profit from the information they have obtained and the decisions they have made.

B. **You finance his fleet of three ships, realizing that you're going to have to sell the family jewels to do so. 1 point.** A big gamble. You know the odds are long, so there are only a limited number of ways to justify this decision. You must either be convinced that the potential payoffs are so large as to justify the risk, or the marginal value of the jewels you will sell must be so small as to make the potential risk relatively small. You might also justify this move from the standpoint of discovering a short route to Asia before your rivals do.

C. **You give him partial support by supplying him with enough funds for one ship to get him started. −1 point.** This is a situation in which if you are in for a penny, you'd better be in for a pound. An investor who puts up 51 percent of the capital only puts up a little more capital than someone who puts up 49 percent, but he or she gets to run the show. If you decide to participate as a minority investor, you need to negotiate in advance the share that you will receive of the total payoff so you can determine whether it is a worthwhile investment. There is also the danger that you might be the only backer, and Columbus tries to discover America with just the *Pinta* (or the *Niña* or the *Santa Maria*). One of the reasons that several ships often undertook these voyages together was that if one ship sunk, the others could carry on. But, if there's only one ship, there are no others.

WHAT ACTUALLY HAPPENED

We Americans have good reason to be delighted that Queen Isabella chose to subsidize Columbus's expedition. However, the hoped-for profits from finding a short route to Asia did not materialize during her reign, and the discovery of America was simply a fortunate spin-off from an otherwise marginal decision.

What You Can Learn from History

The probability of two things both happening is generally less than the probability of just one thing happening; each time something else has to happen in order for a situation to work out favorably, it's that much less likely that it will. In the previous quiz, it wasn't a slam dunk that the world was round—some people felt that if you strayed too far, you'd sail off the edge of the world. From Isabella's standpoint, they might have been right. Also, even if the world were round, Columbus was planning to go where no man had gone before—a risky venture, even before "Star Trek."

A Brief Excursion into Probability Theory

As was mentioned earlier, mathematicians view the probability scale as going from 0 to 1. If two events are independent—the outcome of one having no effect on the outcome of the other—the probability of both events happening is obtained by multiplying the probabilities of each event separately. For instance, if you flip a fair coin, the probability of the coin landing heads is ½, and if you draw a card from a deck of cards, the probability that the card is a spade is ¼. If you both flip a coin and draw a card, the probability of the coin landing heads *and* the card being a spade is ½ × ¼ = ⅛.

That rule can be adapted for situations in which the numbers are less accurately determined. If one thinks of probabilities as belonging to one of three levels of likelihood—"likely," "maybe," and "unlikely"—the probability of any two events both occurring, one of which is unlikely, is just about impossible. A reasonable rule of thumb is that the probability of any two events both occurring each of which is separately either "likely" or "maybe" is one level of likelihood down from the lower of the two. Using this framework, the probability of two "likely" events both happening is a "maybe" event.

Another point in making good decisions, which we will examine in more detail later in the book, is the importance of using information. The noted author Damon Runyon once said that the battle isn't always to the strong, nor the race to the swift—but that's the way to bet. Similarly, experts are sometimes wrong, but they're the equivalent of the strong and the swift in their areas of expertise. One of the major factors in the advance of civilization is the accumulation of expertise. Take medicine, for instance. Would you rather trust your health to your internist—or a majority vote of the U.S. Senate or the Academy of Motion Picture Arts and Sciences?

Of course, when one is flying blind, as Isabella was, there are no experts; neither the king of Portugal nor the Spanish commission to whom Columbus first tried to sell the idea qualified as an expert in the shape of the Earth. Yet each reached the conclusion that this wasn't a reasonable venture. The probability (that word again) of both being wrong is substantially less than the probability of just one of them being wrong. So there were two perfectly valid reasons for Isabella not to finance the venture. Sometimes the wrong decision turns out to be the winner.

Engine Trouble

The assembly line certainly didn't start with you, Henry Ford. It traces its ancestry back to the manufacture of muskets for the American Revolution. Even before that, Venetian shipbuilders used canals as their moving "belt." On the other hand, you are certainly the one individual most responsible for raising the assembly line to the level of an art form. Since you quit automobile racing a few years ago to devote yourself full-time to the manufacture of automobiles, it has been your stated goal to bring the cost of producing automobiles down to the point where anyone with a good salary would be able to afford one. This goal may produce a revolution in transportation that turns out to be as significant an advance as any in history. Unfortunately, as your first Model Ts roll off the production line in October 1908, a fly appears in the ointment. It's the Selden patent, which its holders—who are not you—claim gives them a wide measure of control over the production of internal combustion engines. Other manufacturers evidently concur, as they've signed restrictive licensing agreements with the patent holders. You see the patent as a potential obstacle to open industry development, but you've got a business to run. Do you feel it is best to

A. **go along with the other manufacturers and obtain a licensing agreement so you can at least maintain parity with them?**

B. **take the holders of the patent to court, attempting to obtain a legal victory that would open up progress of the automobile industry?**

C. **invest in some top designers to "reverse engineer" your way around the restrictions of the patent?**

SOLUTIONS: *Engine Trouble*

A. **You go along with the other manufacturers and obtain a licensing agreement so you can at least maintain parity with them. 1 point.** The good news is that you are certain to avoid the disaster of going out of business. However, the licensing agreements are restrictive, and not only will they prevent you from manufacturing the car that you want to manufacture, but they may make the car that you do manufacture too expensive for the mass market.

B. **You take the holders of the patent to court, attempting to obtain a legal victory that would open up progress of the automobile industry. 5 points.** Although it is never clear in advance what your probability of winning a given legal battle may be, the payoffs here are so large that this is your best action. *Even if you can't estimate the probability of success, if the payoffs are large, it's generally right to pursue success as long as it doesn't seem like a hopelessly long shot.*

C. **You invest in some top designers to "reverse engineer" your way around the restrictions of the patent. 2 points.** While this may be a reasonable approach, it is 1908, and there aren't that many top designers around. You may want to adopt this action after your legal expedients are exhausted, but for now it is better to invest in good lawyers than in good engineers, as the payoffs are higher from a legal victory than from an engineering victory.

WHAT ACTUALLY HAPPENED

Ford finally won a long legal fight in 1911, a development that eventually led to the realization of Ford's dream. In 1911 Model

Ts sold for $500, and fifteen years later much better cars were even cheaper. This victory was seen by the public as a triumph for the little man over the monopolies, and for years Ford was the top producer of automobiles in America.

What You Can Learn from History

Virtually any course of action with reasonable probabilities of success and large payoffs is worth pursuing. If you're a guy, it's probably not worth spending your time mooning over Angelina Jolie (*very* low probability), but if you're in reasonable shape and not seriously in debt, you'd be surprised how many girls will at least go out with you on a first date—including ones you may not think would give you the time of day. High payoffs, remember? Incidentally, I saw this advice in a book back in the 1960s—the author didn't cite decision theory, but the advice was good. Take a deep breath, pick up the phone, and remember the high payoffs. If you do this several times, the laws of probability guarantee one of two things—either you'll have a date, or you are much more out of shape than you may think.

CHAPTER 5 Dumping the Losers

The Admissibility Criterion

There are four major decision criteria in decision theory, and these criteria, or standards on which a decision may be based, can be used in a wide range of scenarios. In this chapter, we will tackle the first of the Big Four, the *admissibility criterion*. Let's begin the discussion of admissibility with a situation that has probably come up about five million times—and that's just in the last year. It certainly did to me when I was younger.

Getting Wheels

Despite the fact that you're only the third-string running back on your high school football team, you've still managed to score an unbelievable coup by bagging a date with Lydia Macintosh (yes, *the* Lydia Macintosh!) for Friday night, just three short days from now. Now, however, you are faced with that classic logistical problem: transportation. This is critical; the Lydia Macintoshes of the world don't go on second dates with guys who take the bus. It's a standard problem for a teenage boy in a typical American family; you have to talk your parents into letting you have the family car. Ordinarily, this wouldn't be a major hassle, but they're pretty steamed about that C minus on your last algebra exam, and Friday is fast approaching. After some reflection, you have narrowed your possible actions to the following three choices. Should you

A. **ask your father, because he basically makes the decision as to who gets the car and when?**
B. **ask your mother, the romantic of the family?**
C. **ask both of them simultaneously, say at dinner, when everyone's feeling pretty good after a good meal?**

SOLUTIONS: *Getting Wheels*

The quizzes in this section involve realizing that sometimes alternatives can be eliminated simply on the grounds that another alternative will always result in higher payoffs. Alternatives that can be eliminated in this fashion are referred to as *inadmissible*. Take a look at the analysis for alternative A to see how this applies.

A. **You ask your father, because he basically makes the decision as to who gets the car and when. 1 point.** If you can get his approval, you're home free. But can you? See if you can think of a situation in which Dad will approve but Mom will say no. Pretty tough, isn't it? This tells you that, in all possible cases, the payoffs, which in this case are the success percentages for you getting the car, for asking Dad are less than the payoffs for asking Mom.

B. **You ask your mother, the romantic of the family. 5 points.** In a typical family, mothers are more likely than fathers to stick up for the son. Especially in matters of the heart, Mom is almost certain to say "yes" every time Dad says "yes," and Mom will say "yes" in situations where Dad won't. As a result, asking Dad is inadmissible when compared with asking Mom. *Adopting an inadmissible option is like accepting exactly the same job for lower pay—it's an absolute no-no.* Additionally, that C minus puts you in a vulnerable position, and so you've got to focus on your opponent's weakness rather than your strength. Dad may control the keys to the car, but Mom generally controls the keys to Dad, and if Mom says "yes," Dad will have a hard time overruling her.

C. **You ask both of them simultaneously, say at dinner, when everyone's feeling pretty good after a good meal. 3 points.** Once again, the payoffs for asking Mom dominate the payoffs for asking both of them. Getting a "yes" from both of them just has to be tougher than simply getting a "yes" from Mom, no matter how good the meal is. You're liable to see each glance at the other and hear a remark such as "We'll think about it." Even so, you've at least brought Mom into the picture before Dad has a chance to say "no."

Admissibility

Eliminating inadmissible alternatives, those that have inferior payoffs on a case-by-case basis when compared with another

By the Numbers

The admissibility criterion is easily grasped when presented using numerical payoffs. Suppose that a doctor is faced with a difficult diagnosis and cannot decide whether a patient has one of two different diseases—let's call them Ebola and bird flu. Suppose that she has two drugs at her disposal—megamycin and supercillin. Let's suppose that the cure percentages are given by the following table.

	EBOLA	BIRD FLU
Megamycin	70	40
Supercillin	50	30

Supercillin is seen to be inadmissible—if the patient has Ebola, megamycin cures it 70 percent of the time as opposed to 50 percent for supercillin, and similarly, megamycin is also more effective against bird flu.

Unfortunately, not every decision that involves inadmissibility comes with a printed numerical table, known as a *payoff matrix*, such as this. Sometimes you have to reason your way through it—as in the following situation.

action, is a commonsense decision principle and is often the easiest and most intuitive way to apply decision theory to your day-to-day life. A simple example would be when you're signing up for a health plan. If the features that are important to you are cost and doctor accessibility and plan A is cheaper than plan B and gives you access to more and equally competent doctors, there's not a chance in hell that you'll choose plan B.

Sixteen and Scared

You and your best friend are sixteen—and she's never been so scared in her life, because she's pregnant. Yes, she's sure—she went to two different stores, bought two different pregnancy tests, and they both turned out positive. She's not the first girl to encounter this situation, maybe not even the millionth, but she has no idea what to do, so she decided to seek your advice. She tried a teen-help hotline, but the impersonality turned her off—she had no idea whether she was talking to someone who really cared or someone ticking off questions (and advice) from a preprepared list. She needs to talk to someone who can help her make the right decision *and* keep it under her hat until the situation is resolved. She's settled on talking to one of the three people whom she trusts the most. The only question is—which one?

- **A. Her mother, who has been both a mom and a friend but almost certainly didn't expect something like this to happen.**
- **B. The school counselor, who has a reputation as a cold fish but whom everyone trusts.**
- **C. Your mother, who has always regarded her as if she were her own daughter.**

SOLUTIONS: *Sixteen and Scared*

A. You advise your friend to talk to her mother, who has been both a mom and a friend but almost certainly didn't expect something like this to happen. 1 point. If she wants love, compassion, and sympathy, this is unquestionably where she should go. But are those really her payoffs? What she wants is good advice. This will be a huge shock for her mother, and you can't be sure how good her advice will be when she's under stress. Just as important, how will your friend break the news?

B. **You tell her to go see the school counselor, who has a reputation as a cold fish but whom everyone trusts. 5 points.** You can be sure of one thing—your friend is not the first girl in your high school to come to her with this problem. The school counselor has undoubtedly encountered lots of girls in this situation and not only has training but experience. She won't tell your friend what to do, but she will tell her what her options are, and how to talk to the people involved. She'll also give her some good tips on how to break the news to her family—and anyone else, if it comes to that. This alternative is also best because if you look down the road, your friend will almost certainly have to discuss the situation with her mother and may discuss it with your mother as well. The school counselor is well positioned to help her deal as effectively as possible with the other people in the drama.

C. **You recommend she talk to your mother, who has always regarded her as if she were her own daughter. −1 point.** There are two sets of payoffs here, helpfulness and confidentiality. Talking to the school counselor has to be more helpful, in the sense of being informative and objective, than talking to either parent. From the standpoint of confidentiality, talking to her mother is better than talking to your mother—after all, your mother will consider talking to her mother, but it's unlikely that her mother will consider talking to your mother. The admissibility criterion therefore eliminates your mother from the picture—no matter how close your friend's relationship with her has been in the past.

The principle of eliminating inadmissible alternatives is a natural one. The difficulty is that it's not always immediately clear that one alternative is inadmissible when compared to another one. In order to determine this, it is necessary to look down the road a little and try to list the different situations that may occur. This isn't always easy to do. The young lady whose predicament formed the subject matter of the preceding quiz might have run quickly to her friend's mother, fearing the wrath of her own mother and not being comfortable confiding in the school counselor. She wouldn't be the first to select an alternative that reflection reveals as inadmissible.

In order to determine whether an alternative is inadmissible, you have to be very clear on what your payoffs are. In *Men Are from Mars, Women Are from Venus*, John Gray discusses the idea that men see problems as broken toasters that need fixing and women see them as opportunities to increase the closeness of the support group. These are obviously different payoff systems.

Learning Experiences

We often hear it said that a particular event was a learning experience. Virtually every unsatisfactory outcome provides us with learning experiences—but successful outcomes do as well, giving us greater and greater insight as to how and when to apply the inadmissibility criterion. Both pain and pleasure afford us opportunities for learning experiences—but most of us learn mainly from our unsuccessful experiences, especially if they are so unsuccessful that the pain associated with failure makes a lasting impact on us. One of the reasons that the admissibility criterion is such a useful one is that it's not subtle. It's usually easy to see in retrospect that we selected an alternative that was inferior to another one in all conceivable circumstances. It's very much like the poker player who remembers those situations in which he was "drawing dead"—meaning even if he made his best possible draw, he was doomed to lose.

There's a well-known saying that if you feed a man a fish, you've provided him with a meal, but if you teach the man how to fish, you've given him a way to feed himself and his family. Faced with the choice of accepting a meal or fishing lessons, fishing lessons win out on the admissibility criterion; this alternative not only solves the present problem, but it helps solve other problems that may occur in the future. Most of us are near-term oriented. When we have a problem, we deal with that problem, and that's that. It's certainly worth spending a little extra time to see if there's a solution that not only deals with the problem at hand but problems down the road as well. The fishing lessons give future payoffs as well as present ones, and future payoffs should always be considered when making a decision.

The Loan Arranger

Your wife calls you "Dizzy," but your name is Benjamin Disraeli, and you are prime minister of England. For years, you have been trying to find a way to guarantee access by sea to India, the British Empire's most important possession. Suddenly, an opportunity has arisen. The khedive of Egypt is in hock up to his eyeballs, and Egypt's shares in the Suez Canal are on the market. This is the opportunity you have been waiting for, but there are problems. You have it on good authority that the khedive is at this moment negotiating with French financiers. In order to beat them to the punch, you need four million pounds, and you need it *yesterday*! Parliament is not in session at the moment, so you can't obtain the money through the usual governmental channels, and any move you make must be kept completely secret, otherwise the French financiers will realize the necessity of closing the deal quickly. A quick review of your options makes you realize that there are only three actions with any chance of success, and you've got to pick one and go with it. Should you

A. **contact Baron Lionel de Rothschild, one of the world's richest men, with whom you are well acquainted, and try to get him to float the loan?**
B. **get word to Queen Victoria, with whom you are on excellent terms, and tell her that she must help you convene an extraordinary session of Parliament to fund this venture?**
C. **contact a consortium of British bankers who can put together a sufficiently large pool of capital?**

SOLUTIONS: *The Loan Arranger*

A. **You contact Baron Lionel de Rothschild, one of the world's richest men, with whom you are well acquainted, and try to get him to float the loan. 5 points.** Your payoffs are measured in speed, probability of success, and secrecy. It is reasonable to assume that, as prime minister of the most powerful nation on Earth, you have enough clout to ensure success, so it comes down to a matter of speed and secrecy. The fewer the parties involved, the greater will be both the speed and the secrecy.

B. **You get word to Queen Victoria, with whom you are on excellent terms, and tell her that she must help you convene an extraordinary session of Parliament to fund this venture. −2 points.** Even though the combined powers of the queen and the prime minister are virtually certain to be able to convene such a session, by the time it gets done, the deal will have gone up in smoke. Besides, it's going to be pretty hard to keep this deal a secret when there are hundreds of MPs (members of Parliament) involved.

C. **You contact a consortium of British bankers who can put together a sufficiently large pool of capital. 1 point.** While this would not be an unreasonable approach, the payoffs for this action are dominated in both speed and secrecy by an approach to Baron de Rothschild. *Once your payoff structure has been determined, look carefully at your alternatives—it may be possible to eliminate one (or more) simply on the basis that its payoffs are inferior to those of another action.*

WHAT ACTUALLY HAPPENED

Disraeli, who was unable to meet with de Rothschild personally, sent his secretary to put the bite on the baron. Rothschild, who was at lunch, swallowed a grape and then asked, "What's your security?" The reply was, "The British government." The loan was approved, and Britain obtained control of the vital Suez Canal. British military control of the Suez Canal was eventually turned over to Egypt in 1956.

What You Can Learn from History

If you only have time for one shot, make it your best shot. However, if you are not so pressed, you can often learn from the shots you miss. A job applicant with several interviews should try to arrange to have the last interview with the most desirable company because a lot can be learned from the earlier interviews about the interview process. In fact, most of us have grasped this decision theory concept in an important area of our lives—dating.

CHAPTER 6

Worst-Case Scenarios

The Minimax Criterion

Perhaps the single most influential book in mathematical economics is the classic *Theory of Games and Economic Behavior* by John von Neumann and Oskar Morgenstern. *Game theory,* an investigation of the best strategy to pursue when there is an adversary whose interests oppose yours, has its origins in this groundbreaking work. We shall investigate game theory in later chapters, but one of the early results in this field was the *minimax theorem* (which states that in a game in which one player wins what the other loses, rational play by both players results in a long-term average gain by one of the players), about which von Neumann said, "I thought there was nothing worth publishing until the minimax theorem was proved." Although the minimax criterion first was formally stated in connection with game theory, it was soon realized that one didn't have to have a formal opponent for the criterion to be useful—as in the following situation.

Class Outing

About once every three or four years, you get an absolutely outstanding sixth-grade class, and teaching them this year has been a delight. You've each learned from one another—they've learned long division and literature; you've learned about Hannah Montana. You were a little worried that you might miss the upcoming class outing a few weeks hence when you had to go into the hospital for observation, but after a battery of EKGs and similar tests, the medics couldn't find anything wrong and let you go back to work with just a warning to take it easy. You've followed their advice and gotten a lot of rest, and you're ready to finish off the school year in style and enjoy a well-earned summer vacation. However, you still have to decide where to go for the class outing, as it's up to you to break a three-way tie among

- **A. a trip to Disneyland, the Magic Kingdom that its publicity agents tell you is the happiest place on Earth.**
- **B. a trip to the beach, just the ticket on those hot summer days that seem to start just around the end of the school year.**
- **C. a baseball game, which despite the inroads made by basketball and football, is still the national pastime.**

SOLUTIONS: *Class Outing*

The key to analyzing this decision is that you don't want to end up in the hospital—or worse. The minimax criterion, the subject of this chapter, involves making decisions from the standpoint of avoiding the worst-case scenario.

A. **You decide to take the kids to Disneyland, the Magic Kingdom that its publicity agents tell you is the happiest place on Earth. −1 point.** The Magic Kingdom could turn out to be a nightmare for someone who has been given a battery of tests that figure to be related to heart trouble. You are in a situation in which you are looking for the least potential risk, and even if only the kids go on those souped-up roller coasters, you could easily get overexcited simply watching them.

B. **You cast your deciding vote for a trip to the beach, just the ticket on those hot summer days that seem to start just around the end of the school year. 5 points.** This figures to be just the ticket for you as well as for them. Remember, your primary goal is to avoid disaster—both for your kids and, more importantly, for you. The beach is a relaxing environment, and part of the worry about watching over what the kids are doing will be taken over by the lifeguards. Relax. Enjoy.

C. **You decide to take them to a baseball game, which despite the inroads made by basketball and football, is still the national pastime. 2 points.** This doesn't figure to cause too many problems, but what if the game is close, or the pitcher has a no-hitter going, or the kids eat too much junk food and get hyper? In the heat of battle, you may find yourself eating too much junk food and getting hyper as well. *When you decide you want to minimize your risks, you must make sure you know exactly what the worst outcomes are for each possible alternative. If you don't know what the worst-case scenario is for each alternative, how can you be expected to choose the least dangerous one?*

The Minimax Criterion

"Minimax," as you might expect from the structure of the word and the foregoing quiz, refers to choosing the alternative that *mini*mizes the *max*imum danger. Whenever you see the quarterback of the team that's ahead with only a few seconds left in the game take the snap from the center and kneel down, the minimax criterion is being applied. The only thing that can prevent victory is for the other team to get the ball and have an opportunity to score, and the way to minimize that is for the quarterback not to hand off nor to pass the ball but end the play as soon as possible.

There is a reverse side to the minimax criterion that football, as well as other games, also illustrates. A team that's behind with only a short time left often resorts to desperate maneuvers

---

By the Numbers

Let's take another look at the payoff matrix we encountered in the previous chapter. (As a reminder, the numbers represent the cure percentage for each drug.)

	EBOLA	BIRD FLU
Megamycin	70	40
Supercillin	50	30

Let's suppose that we were to look at the worst that could happen with either of the drugs. If we use megamycin, we might only end up with a cure percentage of 40 percent; similarly with supercillin, we might only end up with a cure percentage of 30 percent.

Based simply on these two numbers, an early advantage accrues to megamycin—its worst-case result is better than the worst-case result from using supercillin.

The minimax criterion is an important decision theory principle—but it is by no means the only club in the bag. It is usually the best principle in cases for which a decision has a reasonable probability of encountering a catastrophic result. An enterprise in its formative stages is a delicate organism—one critically wrong decision can kill it. In such situations, the minimax criterion is extremely useful. Even nature uses the minimax criterion; if birds have two chicks in the nest and food is scarce, the stronger chick gets fed at the cost of starving the weaker one in order to make sure that at least one chick survives.

because it doesn't matter whether the team loses by a little or loses by a lot—a loss is still a loss.

The minimax principle correlates nicely with *risk assessment*—the more you have to lose, the less you can afford to risk, and the converse. As a result, individuals contemplating a financial strategy for a lifetime should be much more willing to make riskier investments when they are young as opposed to when they are approaching retirement. Having spent most of your working lifetime nurturing your nest egg, you want to be *very* sure that the egg you have spent such a long time brooding (and brooding over) will assuredly hatch.

Here's a situation recently encountered by a nationwide chain that almost certainly has a branch near you.

Not So Grande

The original Starbucks was opened in Seattle in 1971 by two teachers and a writer and, after starting life as an ordinary coffee house, expanded into espresso and coffee concoctions. As a result, Starbucks grew like wildfire—at one point in the early 1990s, it was opening an outlet a day, and by 2007, it had nearly fifteen thousand stores, either in its own chain or as joint ventures. However, as food and gasoline prices increased in 2008, people started cutting back—and customers who had been buying $4 Frappuccinos daily are now either switching to plain coffee or coming in only two or three days a week. Something has to be done to prevent a stream of red ink from turning into a torrent. Although Starbucks has been approached by other businesses looking to use the Starbucks stores as an outlet for their merchandise, this does not seem to fit with its corporate image. Its choices seem to be the following:

A. **Closing some of its lowest-performing stores**
B. **Cutting its prices so it can lure customers back and make up the difference in added volume**
C. **Raising its prices on the assumption that it can raise its profit margin while maintaining its customer base**

SOLUTIONS: *Not So Grande*

A. **Its executives decide to close some of its lowest-performing stores. 5 points.** Definitely the best move. The era of frenetic expansion is obviously over—it couldn't be expected to go on forever, otherwise there really would have been a Starbucks on every corner rather than the mere perception that such was the case. *Adverse situations always* *prompt thoughts that things could certainly get worse, and cutting out the weak sisters is an obvious and sensible minimax play.*

B. It cuts its prices so it can lure customers back and make up the difference in added volume. −1 point. There's no guarantee at all that this will work. People are deciding to reduce their Frappuccino habit because by applying their own version of the minimax criterion, they have calculated that there is a major cost savings by doing so. These people probably aren't coming back without a turn in the economy.

C. It raises its prices on the assumption that it can raise its profit margin while maintaining its customer base. −2 points. This is even worse than the previous alternative. Profits are dropping because of increased prices; unless Starbucks's customer base now consists of people who are impervious to a declining economy, raising prices could be catastrophic. Do the math; if Starbucks raises the price 25 cents on a $4 Frappuccino and it loses one customer out of seventeen, it has broken even, not increased its profit. And it has lost a customer in the process. Even if you don't do the math, you only want to make aggressive moves in optimistic situations or absolutely desperate ones—and this is neither.

WHAT ACTUALLY HAPPENED

This one was pretty much a slam dunk; Starbucks closed more than six hundred of its stores in reaction to its financial picture. Starbucks is not only popular but widely watched by financial analysts as a sign of the general health of the economy; when it raised its prices a nickel on every cup of coffee back in September 2006, the move made headlines worldwide. Although it might be coincidence, the profitability (as well as the stock price) of Starbucks has been declining ever since. The possible unwillingness of patrons to cough up that extra nickel might have been viewed as an early harbinger of the coming global hard times. Starbucks almost certainly could have gotten away with such a move had the economy cooperated, but when the price of gasoline started climbing, stock prices and retirement funds started eroding, and people started losing their jobs, expensive cups of coffee didn't seem quite as attractive. When black ink starts turning to red, it's important to prevent a trickle from turning into a torrent. The minimax criterion is applicable in such cases.

As this book is being written, the American economy is contracting. People are worried about losing their jobs, so they reduce their spending. Businesses are concerned with making sure that they are still in business, so they are looking at moves to stave off potential disaster. Economies are cyclic. Good times are periods of expansion; bad times are periods of stasis or contraction, and minimax moves are favored during them. This applies not only to economies but to the lives of individuals as well.

Hot Potato

Whenever a new executive takes over a job, he or she likes to bring in his or her own management team, and you, John F. Kennedy, have certainly brought about wholesale changes in the Washington scene. Nonetheless, experience is a valued commodity, and so you have left Allen Dulles, the brother of Dwight Eisenhower's secretary of state John Foster Dulles, in charge of the CIA. The CIA has a hot potato on its hands. It has been training a brigade of anti-Batista and anti-Castro Cubans in Guatemala. The general idea is that they are preparing to invade Cuba, take over a few radio stations, and rally the Cubans to their cause, which is to get rid of Fidel Castro. Allen Dulles tells you that if you refuse to support this plan, not only will you look like a wimp, but there's a chance that the CIA trainees will divulge the plan to other Cubans and (shudder) the media as well. Some of the more zealous anti-Communists want you to support the invasion with an American air strike, which makes you wonder how good their chances are if they are left to their own devices. It looks as if the more military support you give, the better their chances for success, but also the greater the potential political fallout from messing around trying to overthrow foreign governments. Is it better to be safe or sorry? Should you

A. **pull the plug on the entire invasion operation?**
B. **do your best to ensure the success of the invasion by supporting it with American air power?**
C. **wish the Cubans luck but have them go it on their own?**

SOLUTIONS: *Hot Potato*

A. **You pull the plug on the entire invasion operation.**
5 points. If you let the invasion proceed, you'd better make sure it succeeds. If the invasion fails, you will have egg on your face for supporting it, no matter what the extent of your support. If the invasion succeeds, it is unlikely that the CIA's role can remain hidden. You will be accused of meddling in affairs that are none of your business, although this will be a small price to pay for success. By scuttling the operation, you are choosing the minimax action. *Whenever you start a new enterprise, it's generally better not to attempt really risky maneuvers unless you are trying to prevent the ship from sinking.*

B. **You do your best to ensure the success of the invasion by supporting it with American air power.**
2 points. This gives you the greatest chance of having the

invasion succeed, but if it fails *despite* your support, you will suffer not only a massive military defeat but a public relations setback as well. And don't forget the fact that the Russians are big fans of the Castro government. This action therefore entails the largest possible negative payoffs and so is the worst from a minimax standpoint.

C. **You wish the Cubans luck but have them go it on their own. −2 points.** If the Cubans pull it off, the gains from ridding Cuba of Castro will more than compensate for the whispering campaign that you will hear when the rumors of CIA involvement start. If they fail, your payoffs are going to be negative. The problem is that their chance of success is small compared to action B, yet this action retains the downside negative payoffs of action B with a higher probability of realizing those negative payoffs.

WHAT ACTUALLY HAPPENED

Kennedy fumbled this one by deciding to let the Cubans go ahead on their own. The resulting disaster at the Bay of Pigs was the first major setback for the new administration. An aftermath of the failure to remove Castro was the buildup of Soviet missiles in Cuba. This resulted in the Cuban missile crisis, one of the pivotal events of the Cold War.

What You Can Learn from History

In any new enterprise, unless there's an overwhelming need for drastic action, it's always a good idea to get your feet wet while learning what works and what doesn't, so the minimax criterion is a good one to apply for new ventures. Potential disasters can occur during the early portion of the learning curve. That's why a first date is usually on the order of coffee and conversation rather than a limo, a luxury restaurant, and front-row tickets to the hottest show in town.

Nothing Ventured, Nothing Gained

This may sound funny coming from a numbers guy, but most aphorisms, such as "Nothing ventured, nothing gained," are extremely valuable if they are applied at the right time. If they are applied at the wrong time, they are disastrous. When contemplating any sort of endeavor, it is important to assess the possible rewards *and* the possible risks and to judge whether it is more important to pursue rewards or to abjure risks.

In "Like a Rolling Stone," Bob Dylan opined, "When you ain't got nothing, you got nothing to lose." Nicely—and concisely—put. The time to take large risks is when there is very little downside to loss. Conversely, the minimax principle urges us to tread warily when we have a lot to lose.

CHAPTER 7

In the Long Run

The Bayes' Criterion

H ere's an opportunity to see how you would have made one of history's most famous and important decisions.

Fat Man and Little Boy

It was a lot easier, Harry Truman, when you were vice president. But less than three months after you assumed the vice presidency, Franklin D. Roosevelt died, and the responsibility of directing the American war effort fell on your shoulders. It's all over in Europe now, but there is still the matter of finishing the war against Japan. A massive invasion of the Japanese homeland has been planned for the fall, and from what your generals tell you, it could cost up to a million American casualties. To use an analogy from one of your favorite activities, poker, a wild card has suddenly entered the game. The Manhattan Project, a four-year effort of which you only recently have become aware, has resulted in a successful test of an atomic bomb in the New Mexico desert. Even though you may have only just learned about it, the recent conference at Yalta made you suspicious that Stalin already was aware of it—possibly some sort of a leak had taken place. There are only two atomic bombs in the American arsenal, Fat Man and Little Boy, and it's up to you to decide how to use them. There's no guarantee that they will even work—test conditions cannot simulate actual war conditions. Should you

- **A. figure that because you can win the war by conventional means, it would be a good idea to hide these aces to play in some future war if it becomes necessary?**
- **B. drop them on Japanese cities in the hope of forcing the Japanese to surrender and eliminate the need for an invasion, with the tremendous loss of life that would entail?**
- **C. heed the advice of some of your scientists and arrange for a nonmilitary demonstration of the weapon to the Japanese, which the scientists feel would not only force Japan to surrender but would save the lives of the innocent civilians in the target Japanese cities?**

SOLUTIONS: *Fat Man and Little Boy*

The Bayes' Criterion, the third of the Big Four decision criteria discussed in this book, involves selecting the alternative that will produce the greatest long-term gain. The long-term gain involves the mathematical concept of *expected value*, a key idea in any decision in which there are several potential outcomes with varying probabilities of occurrence—and varying rewards associated with that outcome.

A. You figure that because you can win the war by conventional means, it would be a good idea to hide these aces to play in some future war if it becomes necessary. −3 points. You are going to win the war, so the payoffs of any decision must be measured in the expenditure of the lives of your troops. When measured in lives, the payoff of this strategy seems to be −1,000,000, and the probability of achieving that payoff is very high. Almost anything would be preferable.

B. You drop them on Japanese cities in the hope of forcing the Japanese to surrender and eliminate the need for an invasion, with the tremendous loss of life that would entail. 5 points. Even though future historians may not agree, this is a clear-cut decision. If it works, you will save untold American lives. If it doesn't, you can always go ahead with the planned invasion. All you will have lost will be the dubious value of keeping something secret that may not even be a secret anymore, as obviously there are a lot of people working on the Manhattan Project who know what the project is all about.

C. You heed the advice of some of your scientists and arrange for a nonmilitary demonstration of the weapon to the Japanese, which the scientists feel would not only force Japan to surrender but would save the lives of the innocent civilians in the target Japanese cities. −2 points. There is a chance that this strategy may end the war with the absolute minimum loss of life. On the other hand, by letting your opponent see your hand, you are allowing the complications of game theory to enter. Just to consider one horrifying possibility, what if you try a demonstration, the bomb fails to detonate, and the Japanese somehow recover the bomb?

WHAT ACTUALLY HAPPENED

This is perhaps the most second-guessed decision in history. From the standpoint of decision theory, it may have been one of the most straightforward. The demonstration option is inadmissible when compared with the use option, and the use option is far superior to the "save it for a rainy day" option from the standpoint of the decision principle that involves choosing the alternative with the greatest long-term payoffs.

What You Can Learn from History

Hopefully, none of your decisions will ever have as much on the line as this one, but there's a lot you can learn from Harry Truman. *See if you can decide what your payoffs are—sometimes an apparently muddled decision gets clarified by realizing that there is a single quantity that you are seeking to either maximize or minimize.* Not all decisions can be boiled down to deciding the payoff structure, but if that is possible, it usually enables a straightforward comparison among the various options.

The Bayes' Criterion

Thomas Bayes was an eighteenth-century British mathematician and statistician who did important work in the area of probability theory. His greatest contributions involved Bayes' Theorem, which is a little messy technically but is the mathematical foundation for paternity testing and forensic DNA analysis. He also contributed to the investigation of *expected value*, which is the long-term average payoff from choosing a particular alternative when the outcome is uncertain. The Bayes' Criterion comes into play in situations in which it is important to choose the alternative that will result in the greatest payoff over the *long* run.

By the Numbers

The mathematical procedure for computing the *expected value* (the long-term average gain) requires knowing the probabilities of the various outcomes and the payoffs associated with them.

Here's a straightforward example. If you go to Las Vegas, a roulette wheel has thirty-seven numbers (1 through 36), zero, and double zero (00)—38 slots into which a rolling ball can fall. The house takes special care to see that the wheel is properly balanced so that the ball has an equal probability ($\frac{1}{38}$) of rolling into each slot. The house pays 35 to 1 if you bet on a particular number and the ball rolls into that slot, so let's say you bet $10 on your lucky number. There are two outcomes, win and lose. Here's a table to summarize the information you need.

OUTCOMES	PROBABILITY	PAYOFF
Win	$\frac{1}{38}$	+$350
Lose	$\frac{37}{38}$	−$10

To compute the expected value E of a single bet, we multiply the probabilities by the payoffs and add up the result.

$$E = (\tfrac{1}{38}) \times (+\$350) + (\tfrac{37}{38}) \times (-\$10) = -\$0.53$$

Your long-term average payoff from your $10 bet is a loss of $0.53. You can see this another way—if you spin the wheel 38 times and

continued

each of the 38 different numbers comes up once (in accordance with the probabilities), you have a net loss of $20 in 38 spins, or an average loss of $0.53 per spin. That's how they can afford those (relatively) cheap buffets and room rates.

Applying the Bayes' Criterion in the real world is not necessarily clear-cut, because it involves an estimation of probabilities. In the situation Truman faced, for example, there was certainly the possibility that the Japanese were secretly considering surrendering, and the devastation caused by the atomic bomb might have galvanized them to abandon these plans. If that were the case, the atomic bomb would have prolonged the war instead of bringing it to a quick close, and simply waiting for the Japanese to surrender would have resulted in the smallest loss of American life. However, the best guess at the time was that this was an extremely unlikely situation.

The next decision is nowhere near as momentous as Harry Truman's but probably occurs millions of times a year—and that's just in California.

On the Rebound

You weren't a good enough dancer to make a career of it, but it has always been your passion. Not only did it provide you with an activity from which you derived considerable pleasure, it also provided you with a husband. You met him at a local dance studio, and after a whirlwind courtship, the two of you boarded a jet for Vegas, found a chapel, and got hitched. Unfortunately, it turned out to be a lot easier to dance with your husband than live with him. You both tried your best, but after a couple of years, incompatibilities evolved into irreconcilable differences, culminating in divorce. You've spent some time licking your wounds, but you feel that it's time to get back into circulation. You're still young, and you'd like to find your soul mate. After briefly considering and rejecting Internet dating as too risky, three options present themselves. Any of them could work, but rather than spread yourself thin, you've decided to start with just one. Should you

A. put out the word to friends and family that you're on the lookout?
B. figure that it worked before and find different dance events to attend?
C. decide that dancing is best pursued as a hobby and look for love by either going to new places or taking up new activities?

SOLUTIONS: *On the Rebound*

A. You decide to put out the word to friends and family that you're on the lookout. 1 point. The upside here is that if it works out well, it will work out *really* well for everyone involved. You'll have found your soul mate and will make whomever fixed you up with the winner feel especially good. However, there's just too much downside here for this to be the right decision. Your friends and family may think they know what you want, but they could get it extremely wrong—and relationships on all sides could become strained. Finally, it's probably better to wait to hear someone say, "I know someone that I think would be just right for you," than to say to someone, "Do you know anyone you think would be just right for me?"

B. You figure that it worked before and find different dance events to attend. 5 points. You're playing on your home field here; dancing is an activity you enjoy, so you'll meet people who have this in common with you. Additionally, you meet a lot of people this way. *The Bayes' Criterion is about maximizing your long-term payoffs.* Since you can't be sure which approach will find Mr. Right, this way you can maximize the throughput of Mr. Could-Be-the-Ones.

C. You decide that dancing is best pursued as a hobby and look for love by either going to new places or taking up new activities. 2 points. Although this option allows you to do the choosing (as opposed to letting family and friends fix you up), you're simply not going to be able to get the numbers by adopting this approach. You also can't be sure that the people you meet are going to share something that is important to you. If you were a salesman, you'd go after hot prospects, and you can't be sure that this is where the hot prospects are.

Even though Internet dating was rejected as an option in the previous scenario, the ability of the Internet to transfer large numbers of documents quickly (and mostly without expense) has brought about many changes in how things are done now by people who see the Internet as a way to expedite the Bayes' Criterion. When I was in high school, most students applied to three colleges; now many apply to ten or more. Twenty years ago, it was customary for literary agents to send a manuscript proposal to a favored publisher and wait weeks to hear the result—now agents send proposals via mass e-mails to scores of publishers.

Maximizing long-term payoffs can be done not only by maximizing the *quantity* of payoffs but the *quality* of the payoffs as well. A business selling high-end merchandise, for example, should never expand its inventory by adding merchandise of lesser quality, as whatever revenue can be gained from sales of the lesser-quality merchandise will almost certainly be offset by the diminution of the high-end image. While this might be a good short-term solution to shore up profits and help the bottom line, the long-term payoffs will almost certainly be reduced (unless the store can reconstitute itself as Wal-Mart). The Bayes' Criterion is the reason you never see Timex and Rolex watches simultaneously on display. Although doing so would not reduce the store's payoff from selling a Rolex, a store featuring Rolex watches is unlikely to get walk-in customers who want a Timex watch. Giving shelf space to Timex watches therefore reduces the payoff (profit per unit of shelf space) and also reduces the probability of selling a Rolex, as a customer who sees less expensive watches next to pricey ones might wonder if the Rolex is a knockoff.

Blowout

As one of the directors of Bridgestone, you have a major disaster on your hands. Firestone Tires, one of your subsidiaries, has a long past, but a checkered one. Firestone was a major source of collapsible rubber rafts and floating bridges during World War II. After the war, Firestone decided that a good way to get some publicity was by supplying tires to the winning car at the Indianapolis 500—they won the first one, and a lot of others besides. They even named one of their tires the Firestone 500—but the tire had a lot of problems, causing so many deaths and injuries that the tire was recalled. Firestone Tires has slipped behind Goodyear and Bridgestone as the pre-eminent brands, and things are about to get a lot worse. Ford Explorers and Expeditions, equipped with Firestone tires, have incurred a number of fatal accidents as a result of tire tread separation, and the publicity has been widespread. You have to decide what to do about Firestone Tires. Should you

A. institute an elaborate safety program to make sure that all government tests are passed with flying colors?

B. merge Firestone into Bridgestone, effectively retiring the Firestone name, and emphasize that Bridgestone, along with Goodyear and Michelin, is one of the "Big Three" worldwide in tires?

C. underwrite a major advertising campaign to focus attention on the glorious history of the Firestone brand?

SOLUTIONS: *Blowout*

A. You spearhead instituting an elaborate safety program to make sure that all government tests are passed with flying colors. 1 point. This is certainly a reasonable thing to do to try and regain consumer confidence, but the problem is that the horse is already out of the barn. Truly is it written that an ounce of prevention is worth a pound of cure.

B. You merge Firestone into Bridgestone, effectively retiring the Firestone name, and emphasize that

Bridgestone, along with Goodyear and Michelin, is one of the "Big Three" worldwide in tires. 5 points. Sometimes a corporation, like a doctor, has to bury its mistakes. The vast majority of the public may not even know that Firestone is a subsidiary of Bridgestone. *The Bayes' Criterion applies in a variety of instances, and one of them is when you've got to admit when things have gone sour and not throw good money after bad.*

C. **You underwrite a major advertising campaign to focus attention on the glorious history of the Firestone brand. −1 point.** Nobody is interested in the glory days. Joe Torre won several World Series with the Yankees, but when they continually flamed out in the playoffs, he got the axe. Ever heard the expression "What have you done for me lately?"

WHAT ACTUALLY HAPPENED

Firestone has been merged into Bridgestone and is now known as Bridgestone/Firestone. Firestone tires still exist but are now known as Bridgestone/Firestone tires, but the Firestone history is still touted by Firestone Auto Care centers. As the song says, "Accentuate the positive, eliminate the negative"—and that's basically what Bridgestone has done.

The Bayes' Criterion and the Business World

It has often been remarked that American business focuses too much attention on the quarterly bottom line. Analysts make estimates, companies issue quarterly reports—and the stock price of a company can rise and fall by significant amounts. Even a company with a highly profitable quarter can see its stock price plummet (to the consternation of shareholders) if the profits are less than analysts' projections. As a result, the Bayes' Criterion is probably not applied nearly as frequently as it should be. Sometimes one has to bite the short-term bullet in order to realize the long-term payoffs.

And sometimes companies have to ignore the siren call of short-term payoffs in order to focus on the overall picture. A horrifying object lesson in this particular principle can be seen in the massive failure of the mortgage-lending industry beginning in 2008. For years—even for centuries—home loans were serious business, made by banks, who had thoroughly researched the creditworthiness of the would-be borrowers, to individuals who could afford a down payment of a substantial percentage of the house's value. All that began to change with the emphasis on construction of—and aggressive financing of—affordable housing. Eschewing long-term payoffs for short-term results, borrowers took loans they could not afford, and banks made loans to individuals of dubious creditworthiness, backed up by government institutions with insufficient regard for the safety of the taxpayers' dollars. Sound decision-making principles were ignored by all three groups of participants, and the fallout will undoubtedly be felt for years, if not decades.

CHAPTER 8 # Taking the Plunge

The Maximax Criterion

H istory is cyclic. Good times are followed by bad times—and vice versa. Here's a scenario that might hasten the reappearance of good times.

The Next Big Thing

You decided that a really good way to make a lot of money would be to find something that the world has too much of and transform it into something that the world has too little of. Easier said than done, but your years of effort have resulted in what looks like the next big thing: genetically engineered bacteria that happily munch away on plastic trash bags and excrete methane, which can be processed into fuel. In the lab, it looks like you can spin straw into gold, but it's still a long way from making bags of money—you have to obtain a patent on your bacteria and demonstrate that the process will scale up to commercial levels of production. This is going to require money—but, as they say, it takes money to make money, and you have several choices in financing. Should you

A. maintain control by starting small, selling the methane you can produce with your own financing, and gradually expanding production as the profits from the methane you sell allow?
B. give up 75 percent of the stock to a venture capitalist who will finance the whole project?
C. get a low-interest loan from a bank, which will enable you to start both the patent process and increase your level of production?

SOLUTIONS: *The Next Big Thing*

The *maximax criterion* concerns situations in which you should throw caution to the winds and try to get the most out of a situation that you can. As is so often the case, there are two tasks at hand: concluding that you are confronted by a situation that should be decided using the maximax criterion and then choosing the alternative that will enable you to get the most out of the decision.

A. You maintain control by starting small, selling the methane you can produce with your own financing, and gradually expanding production as the profits from the methane you sell allow. 1 point.
The advantage here is that if you can make bags of money, you will keep all of those bags of money. The disadvantage is that you might be too slow to expand with this option. You may have the next big thing, but what about

the big thing after that? There's a lot of interest in finding cheap sources of energy—people are trying all sorts of approaches. You may have only a short time in which to make as much money as you can—don't waste it.

B. You give up 75 percent of the stock to a venture capitalist who will finance the whole project. 5 points. There are three important points in favor of this approach. First, there's no risk to you. Second, this will enable you to scale up as quickly as possible. Third, and most important, 25 percent of a whole lot of money is a whole lot of money. The maximax principle is to look for the good things that can happen and choose the alternative that will produce the greatest payoffs. *Maximax-motivated decisions, those in which you have an opportunity to make a bundle, generally occur rarely—they're the opportunities that often knock just once.* Strike while the iron is hot.

C. You get a low-interest loan from a bank, which will enable you to start both the patent process and increase your level of production. −1 point. The worst of the three alternatives. No bank will give you anywhere near what the venture capitalist offers, as you're just a start-up, and what if you run into unexpected obstacles? You're still going to have to make the interest payments. This is the only approach that can spin gold into straw.

The Maximax Criterion

It's important to make hay while the sun shines because for most of us, the sun doesn't shine too often. While we're on the subject of platitudes, the saying that opportunity knocks but once should be modified slightly; it may knock many times throughout the course of a lifetime but generally only once in each specific situation.

The previous scenario is an instructive example—and hopefully one that might actually occur sometime in the near future. In making the decision, there are two risks to be considered. The first risk is that you may not get everything out of the situation to which you're entitled. The second, and more critical, risk is that you're not the only bright person on the planet. History is replete with numerous examples of inventions—and discoveries—that occurred to several persons roughly simultaneously. To mention just one, when Charles Darwin returned home from his years in the Galapagos, his notes on his theory of natural selection were not published for several years—possibly because Darwin realized the impact that it might have on the structure of society. However, when friends noted that Alfred Russel Wallace had come to the same conclusion, Darwin realized that it was definitely time to submit his material to a publisher *fast*. This was an opportunity that would knock but once, Darwin seized it, and that's why he, and not Wallace, is recognized as the person responsible for the theory of evolution.

By the Numbers

From a historical standpoint, the maximax criterion seems to have been named in retrospect, probably as a counterpart to the minimax criterion. Perhaps someone will decide to name it the Gekko criterion after Gordon Gekko, the fictional protagonist in the 1987 film *Wall Street* who opined that greed is good. There are indeed times when it is not only good to be greedy, it is wrong not to be.

A major decision for many businesses is whether to expand production. This depends critically on the business environment—more critically on the environment for the firm and the industry to which it belongs, and less so on the national and global business environment, just as you are more likely to be nervous knowing that there's a case of swine flu in your hometown than that there's a case of swine flu in your home state. Let's simplify things and measure payoffs in millions of dollars of profit and loss and look at the following payoff matrix.

		EXPAND PRODUCTION?	
		YES	NO
Business Environment	Good	+100	10
	Bad	−100	20

A maximax decision simply looks for the largest payoff, in this case $100 million, and decides to expand production because that's the way to achieve that payoff. Obviously, there are going to be conditions—such as a good business environment—in which going for the pot of gold makes a lot of sense. Such was the case in the following situation.

Genius Move

You should be patting yourself on the back for a move that, in retrospect, looks like absolute genius. A few years ago, when oil was around $50 a barrel, you took a look into the future and didn't like what you saw: a world dependent on oil from a Middle East that seemed to you increasingly unstable. So you recommended that Southwest Airlines, which had already established itself as a growing and profitable company whose profitability was closely tied to fuel prices, buy a huge quantity of oil futures in the $50-a-barrel range. It's now 2008, oil is closer to $150 a barrel than it is to $100 a barrel, and Southwest Airlines has a sizeable competitive advantage because of its substantially lower fuel costs. However, in this league you're only as good as your last recommendation, and Southwest Airlines wants your advice as to what it should do *now*. Should they

A. **sell their oil futures, take a huge profit, and make the stockholders very, very happy?**

B. **use their price advantage in fuel to expand their operations by enlarging the list of cities that they service and adding more flights to the cities that they already service?**

C. **partner with one of the larger airlines, parlaying its network and your foresightedness in the fuel department in an attempt to create an industry behemoth?**

SOLUTIONS: *Genius Move*

A. **You recommend that they sell their oil futures, take a huge profit, and make the stockholders very, very happy. 1 point.** A profit is not without honor, especially when it's a big profit, but Southwest is an airline, not an oil-futures trading company. What you want to do is use this bonanza to improve your relative position in the industry, which calls for an offensive maximax strategy, not a defensive play like this one.

B. **You advise them to use their price advantage in fuel to expand their operations by enlarging the list of cities that they service and adding more flights to the cities that they already service. 5 points.** If there were ever a time for expansion, this is it. The other airlines are hurting. People still need to fly. Opportunity is not merely knocking on your door, it is using a battering ram. *When you know you have the best hand and you feel sure your opponent is going to call, what other action makes sense besides the maximax play of shoving all your chips into the pot?* You'll probably never get a chance like this again, so take advantage of it.

C. **You counsel them to partner with one of the larger airlines, parlaying its network and your foresightedness in the fuel department in an attempt to create an industry behemoth.** **—2 points.** What can they possibly do for you that you can't do for yourself? Not much, and to make matters worse, you'll have to use your fuel advantage to help them get off the mat. There are times when it is noble to help a weakened opponent, and there are also times when it may not be noble but it is simply in your best interest. Noble actions don't take place in the competitive world of business, and this is most definitely not in your best interest.

WHAT ACTUALLY HAPPENED

As the analysis shows, this is a slam dunk, and Southwest announced its plans to expand in June 2008. Even though fuel prices plummeted in the fall of 2008, Southwest was still in good shape. Prices rose again in 2009.

As we have mentioned, though, there are situations that call for you to look down the road—as in the following scenario.

Second-Stringer

You're a six-foot-three all-state quarterback with an absolute cannon for an arm, so it's not surprising that every football school in the nation was knocking on the door offering you a scholarship and the magazines touted you as a sure shot to make the pros. After mulling the offers over, you went to a school that had won two national championships in the last four years, and where you find yourself in an unaccustomed position—carrying a clipboard sitting on the bench. That's because the coach has stuck with his starting quarterback, a senior without your physical credentials—but the team is winning. The coach has assured you that the job will be yours next year, and he's a man of his word—but he's also offered you the chance to utilize your athletic skills as a defensive back. Coach doesn't realize it, but you are contemplating a third choice. Should you

- **A. stay on the bench and wait for your opportunity?**
- **B. take advantage of coach's offer to play in the defensive backfield?**
- **C. transfer to a second-tier football school where you could immediately be the starting quarterback?**

SOLUTIONS: *Second-Stringer*

A. **You stay on the bench and wait for your opportunity. 5 points.** Your turn will come, and it will come on a great team, where you will be under continual scrutiny. *Maximax decisions are those that demand you strike while the iron is hot—but in some instances, the iron will be just as hot* *a year or two in the future as it is now; this all has to do with analyzing payoffs.* If you've got the stuff of which future NFL quarterbacks are made, you will get to show it, and everyone will know it. Stay the course.

B. **You take advantage of coach's offer to play in the defensive backfield. −1 point.** You didn't come here to play. You came here to be a star quarterback. This would be a huge detour. Look at the negatives—you could get injured, you could lose your quarterbacking skills, or even worse, you could be such a good defensive back that coach finds someone else to quarterback the team.

C. **You transfer to a second-tier football school where you could immediately be the starting quarterback. 2 points.** At least you'll be doing what you do best, but you'll be out of the spotlight on a team that may not enable you to showcase your talents. There is some upside even if you're not surrounded by great talent, because if you can get more out of them than they appear to have, you'll look even better to the pros. Nonetheless, it's easier for a performer to look good if the supporting cast is not muffing their lines.

Sometimes there are situations in which the maximax decision and the Bayes' Criterion decision coincide—as in the previous example. There are instances in which different criteria result in the same decision—although not all roads lead to Rome, sometimes several do.

All too often, though, it's extremely difficult to avoid being seduced by the lure of immediate but lesser payoffs. There's an obvious reason for this—as pointed out by yet another platitude, the one about the bird in the hand being worth two in the bush.

You are giving up the short-term payoffs of immediate quarterbacking for the larger long-term payoffs of quarterbacking a high-profile team. There is a certainty to near-term payoffs that the longer-term payoffs do not have. We live in a world that changes rapidly—the rules of the game often change even as we are playing the game—and so the bird in the hand becomes more than twice as attractive as the two in the bush.

Another obstacle to making good maximax decisions, in addition to succumbing to the lure of short-term payoffs, is an inability to assess exactly which alternative generates the largest payoffs. In the above example, everyone even remotely connected with football knows that the quarterback is, in general, the highest-paid position. However, impressive contracts have also been given to running backs, tight ends, defensive linemen, defensive backs, and even offensive linemen, and the quarterback in the scenario above may think that his best bet is to develop and show skills as a defensive back now since there is a position for him.

There is another type of situation that is best handled using the maximax criterion. If only the largest payoff will achieve your goal, you simply must select the alternative that could generate the largest payoff. In football, even the team with a fabulous running back and a lousy quarterback will throw a "Hail Mary" pass trying for a touchdown near the end of the game if only a quick touchdown can avert defeat.

In general, though, the majority of maximax-motivated decisions are optimistic ones, made in situations that are going well, with the expectation (or at least the hope) that they will get better. Every so often, though, circumstances may conspire to defeat even the best decision. Of the three decisions presented in this chapter, none is impregnable. The genetically engineered bacteria may have been such an incredible long shot that no one else could possibly have produced it, and giving 75 percent of the stock to a venture capitalist is throwing money away. By holding on to the clipboard, the quarterback is risking that another coach with a different philosophy may take over the program or a quarterback with an even better arm will be brought in next year. Southwest Airlines could—and actually did—find the price of fuel plummeting far below the price for which they bought it, and the expansionist move might actually saddle them with bigger losses than had they just stood pat. No one can foresee the future, but it's still best to remember Damon Runyon's words about the way to bet. You can't make winning decisions all the time, but by going with the percentages, you rate to be a big winner in the long run.

Finally, maximax decisions are not always easy for individuals to make but are often just as difficult for organizations—and for all of the reasons cited in this chapter. Additionally, organizations such as governments often have to make a number of decisions, and compromises must be made among the various factions in order to accomplish anything. This difficulty applies not only to maximax decisions but to Bayes' Criterion decisions as well.

CHAPTER 9 Which Club to Use

G olfers know that the choice of club is a critical one. Even when they're on the green, it isn't always right to use the putter. Similarly, the choice of which of the Big Four criteria to use when making a decision is probably the single most important factor in making the correct decision. In this chapter, we shall investigate some guidelines to use in deciding which club to pull out of the bag.

We've all probably made correct decisions using the four criteria we have investigated in the previous chapters without giving any thought to the overall principle of decision making. Almost certainly we've eliminated a clearly weak alternative (admissibility), guarded against a potential disaster (minimax), made a decision we thought would produce the greatest overall returns (Bayes' Criterion), and selected an optimistic alternative that, if successful, would give us the most bang for our buck (maximax). However, it's not enough to simply make a successful decision—we've all done that countless times. The trick is to build upon those successful decisions by focusing on the principles used to make more successful decisions in the future.

Admissibility

The principle that inadmissible alternatives should be avoided is one that is *always* valid. In simple cases in which there is only one system of payoffs under consideration, such as the Groves-Oppenheimer decision, it is usually relatively easy to apply. However, we are frequently confronted by situations in which there are several different payoff systems in play. Should we devote more time to pursuing our career (monetary payoffs) or our social or recreational pursuits (happiness payoffs)? Situations involving different payoff schemes are generally not ones in which we are confronted with inadmissible alternatives. For example, very few of us are faced with the choice of whether we should work in a fast-food restaurant (low monetary, job satisfaction, and happiness payoffs) or star in major motion pictures (probably high payoffs in all three areas). We could easily eliminate the inadmissible alternative here—but the alternative that dominates the admissible one is not a realistic option.

In general, when differing payoff systems are in play, it is necessary to compromise, accepting lower payoffs in one of the systems in exchange for higher payoffs in the other. We shall discuss this in more detail later in the book, but as a rule of thumb, when either differing payoff systems or compromise actions are part of the decision, there will be no inadmissible alternatives to eliminate. As they say in New York, you can be lucky in love, lucky in work, or lucky in real estate or the stock market—but you can't be lucky in all three. You've got to give up payoffs in one area to increase payoffs in another. Such is life.

The Bayes' Criterion

Many decisions come down to a simple choice of which of the three remaining criteria that have been discussed so far— minimax, the Bayes' Criterion, and maximax—is the one to apply. In general, decisions concerning *recurrent situations* are ones that are best made according to the Bayes' Criterion. The fact that a situation recurs means that there is a long term to consider. Minimax decisions are designed to reduce the risk of a disaster; maximax decisions are designed to extract the most profit from opportunity. Staving off disasters or profiting from opportunities are generally unusual events. Something is probably seriously wrong if you find yourself continually staving off disaster, and if you find yourself continually faced with extraordinarily profitable opportunities, please let me in on the action!

This is not to say that the Bayes' Criterion is restricted to those opportunities that recur. The Bayes' Criterion strives to create the greatest average payoff. Averages can be created by recurrent situations, such as batting averages in baseball, but averages can also be created by looking at the probabilities for one-time events, such as the decision to drop the atomic bomb on Japan. Prior to dropping the atomic bomb on Japan, there had been only one test, at the Trinity test site near Alamogordo, New Mexico. It was successful, but only under tightly controlled circumstances. There wasn't sufficient time or resources to do anything other than estimate the probabilities of success under battlefield conditions and the results that might be expected to accrue with success. Nonetheless, even though the atomic bomb was unique, it was simply an example of a situation in which a radical development has a substantial probability of success, with huge payoffs accruing from success. Such situations recur—in business, in history, in our personal lives. Almost always, the Bayes' Criterion answers the question "go or no go" with "go."

Minimax

Minimax decisions, as we know, tend to be made in situations characterized by a disaster that we wish to protect against—and we feel threatened by that potential disaster. Some disasters simply don't threaten us, or we don't feel that the protection is worth the price we have to pay. The first attempt to blow up the World Trade Center took place in 1993, when a truck filled with fifteen hundred pounds of explosives was detonated in an underground garage. In 1995, Timothy McVeigh detonated a truck filled with five thousand pounds of explosives, destroying the Alfred P. Murrah Federal Building, with extensive loss of life. Truck bombs are obviously a potential disaster—but we don't inspect every truck because the probability of their being filled with explosives is so small, and the cost of inspection, in time and money, so overwhelming.

A minimax decision is cautious, conservative—and pessimistic. Nonetheless, there are times when caution and conservatism are advisable. Winston Churchill was reported to have made the sage statement that if you're not a liberal at age twenty, you haven't got a heart, and if you're not a conservative at age forty, you haven't got a brain. Both parts of this remark have implications for decision theory, but for the time being, we'll focus on the part of the quote about being conservative. The accumulation of resources, whether by an individual or an organization, generally comes with age. Neither an individual nor a business wishes to see years of effort and expenditure go up in smoke. However, there is a difference between a business and an individual with regard to the need to make conservative decisions. They both need to protect resources as they mature, but unlike an individual, a business is under constant threat from competition. The adage "grow or die" is basically inapplicable to a mature individual, but many are the enterprises that have faded or vanished because they did not heed this injunction.

Maximax

Because the maximax decision is the one made by choosing the alternative yielding the largest possible payoff, the decision is clearly either an optimistic one—or a desperate one. Optimistic decisions are made when one sees the probability of failure as being very small—in such cases, it obviously makes sense to go for the largest possible payoff. Decisions born of desperation generally fall into the "throw the bomb" category when only the largest payoff will suffice; the term comes from a football team trying a desperation long pass on the last play of the game because it is the only way they can win. The Mafia came to power partially because many people were forced to make maximax decisions; they needed money and could not obtain it in any conventional way, so they would accept the Mafia's terms (borrow five now, pay six next week) to solve their immediate problems. If you need the money for an operation for your child, you get it any way you can and worry about the consequences later.

When Decisions Go Wrong

No one can make all decisions correctly, whether the definition of *correctly* is "the theoretically right decision" or "the one that worked out." It's important, though, to know not only what happens when a decision goes wrong but to be able to figure out that it has gone wrong.

Neither of these situations is a problem with a minimax decision. In general, a badly made minimax decision results in a disaster of some sort. When minimax decisions are successful, it's generally a matter of "no news is good news," and you live to fight another day.

However, it may not be easy to see that a Bayes' Criterion decision, or a maximax decision made from the optimistic viewpoint, has gone awry because in both cases, it is possible to do well. Indeed, it is possible to do very well—and simply not get everything out of the decision that you could have. There are a number of aphorisms that are relevant here, in particular "A rising tide floats all boats." There is a great tendency to become overconfident when things are going well and to think that the good times will continue into the indefinite future. Of course, when the maximax decision is made out of desperation, it is easy to tell when it has gone wrong—but you generally don't second-guess yourself for such a decision because it was the only rational course open to you.

There is also a tendency to ignore the possibility that new developments may alter the landscape. No better case in point could be found than Southwest Airlines's decision to expand because of its fuel-purchasing decision. At the time of the decision, oil was at $140 a barrel, and pundits could be found predicting the imminence of $200-a-barrel oil, with $300-a-barrel oil a real possibility. Who could have foreseen the collapse of the mortgage banking industry, the plunging of the U.S. economy into a severe recession, and the decreased demand for fuel that followed within months? As of this writing, $60 a barrel oil is there for the taking. This does not necessarily invalidate Southwest Airlines's decision, but in an era of financial retrenchment, they may be taking a long, hard look at their expansionary moves.

A Final Word

There are situations for which there are ironclad rules and situations for which there are guidelines. Choosing a decision criterion is a decision for which, unfortunately, there are only guidelines. Part of the reason is that one often finds oneself in situations that cannot be described as black or white, but merely an appropriate shade of gray. For most of our lives, we are not so young that we can afford to make optimistic choices without worrying about the consequences nor so old that we are compelled to make conservative choices in order to protect what we have worked so long to amass. For most of our lives we are somewhere in between—and no one rings a bell to tell you that it's time to switch from optimistically offensive to cautiously defensive.

So what are you to do? Here's a reasonable game plan—with a caveat. All such game plans are so general that they are useful only as an overall guide. Obviously, you have to lay out your alternatives and try to assess the risks and rewards associated with each. Then you see if there are any inadmissible alternatives that can be eliminated. After that has been done, try to assess whether you are clearly in a minimax situation—that's generally fairly obvious, as when disaster looms, it's not a faint cloud on the horizon but a thunderhead. If not, ask yourself how you would react to an alternative not working out; if you can't stand the heat, stay out of the kitchen. This is somewhat reminiscent of the following decision principle: When in doubt, flip a coin. If you are satisfied with the way it landed, accept the decision. If not, eliminate that alternative. Much though we would like decision theory to be an exact science, sometimes there's a gray area. However, if you're really in a gray area, accept the result of the flip of the coin, as in the long run, randomly made decisions in this gray area will at least eliminate the possibility of your habitually making bad decisions—although negating the possibility that you will habitually make good ones.

CHAPTER 10 # What You Don't Know Can Hurt You

O ne of the most important factors in improving one's decision-making abilities is the acquisition and use of information. Information affects a decision by changing the individual payoffs. Changing the payoffs will not alter the way in which a particular strategy is employed, but it can alter the outcome. (Knowing that it will rain tomorrow affects your decision to take an umbrella.) It can also change the choice of strategy. (Tiger Woods plays the eighteenth hole differently depending upon whether he has a lead or not—so you can be sure that either he or his caddy will check out the leaderboard.)

This is the lengthiest chapter in the book because there are aspects to the acquisition and use of information that are not so straightforward as the knowledge of whether it will rain tomorrow or whether you are ahead or behind as you survey the eighteenth fairway.

Let's start with a situation that has launched a thousand advice columns.

Delicate Situation

In the last few days you've been surfing oldies radio stations and you've heard both "Jessie's Girl" by Rick Springfield and "My Best Friend's Girl" by the Cars. Both songs describe your situation—except that something interesting has just happened: your best friend and his girlfriend appear to have broken up. You've admired her both from afar and close up; whenever you've been around the two of them, she and you have conversed fairly comfortably (you've managed to avoid stammering), and it looks like opportunity is knocking. However, it's a delicate situation. He *is* your best friend, and you can't really be sure they've broken up—this may be simply a lovers' spat. As a result, you have eliminated "immediate pounce" from the set of actions you are considering (albeit with some regret) and have narrowed the field to the following three choices.

A. Have an immediate conversation with your best friend, in which you try to learn whether the breakup is final. If he affirms this, you are cleared to launch.

B. Wait for a week or thereabouts. If nothing has happened to bring the unhappy couple together, and you would certainly know, go in with both guns blazing.

C. Wait for a couple of weeks to give time a chance to heal all wounds and pounce if they still fester.

SOLUTIONS: *Delicate Situation*

A. **You have an immediate conversation with your best friend, in which you try to learn whether the breakup is final. Then go for it. 0 points.** You have three different possible alternatives, and there are basically two situations to be considered: they are destined to reunite, or they are destined to remain apart. However, this isn't something that can be determined immediately; you'll get a lot more reliable information if you wait for things to cool down. *Conditions beyond your control (known as* states*) are very much like the weather; you can't do anything to affect them, but you can make better decisions with an accurate forecast.*

B. **You wait for a week or thereabouts and then pursue her with impunity. 5 points.** In the TV series "I Spy" from the 1960s, occasionally such situations would arise, after which one of the protagonists would say to the other, "Go for yourself." If nothing has happened in this period of time, it's time to go for yourself. Your best friend shouldn't expect his girlfriend, or ex-girlfriend, to stay on ice forever, although you might consider discussing this with your BF.

C. **You wait for a couple of weeks to give time a chance to heal all wounds and pounce if they still fester. 2 points.** The only question is whether or not it is better to wait for a longer period of time. It is possible that they could make up with additional waiting time, but it is more likely that the former girlfriend will inaugurate the search for a replacement, and probably sooner than later. You want to know whether you're a candidate before allowing someone else to fill the role.

This scenario is a classic illustration of the value of information in making a decision. It also points out some of the major problems associated with obtaining information.

First, you want to make sure that the information is reliable—it's obviously worse to make a decision based on erroneous information than it is to make a decision based on no information at all. In the above situation, you can be fairly sure that the information you collect over the next week or so will be reliable—especially if your best friend and his girlfriend are seen together.

Second, there is sometimes a cost in obtaining information. In this case, an immediate conversation with your best friend not only is likely to produce no information or unreliable information, it is likely to strain relations between the two of you.

Finally, the value of information is associated with the time at which the information is obtained. A tip on a horse race is useless after the race has been run.

With America's automobile manufacturers currently in considerable disarray, it might be worthwhile to look at a situation that occurred half a century ago.

The '57 Lemon

As a member of the management team of Ford Motor Company, you have helped your firm to rebound from near bankruptcy following World War II to a prosperous number-two position in the domestic market and challenger for number one in the European market. After thorough and intensive market surveys, careful design, and sound and skillful marketing tactics, you have produced in 1957 what is destined to be a legend in the annals of consumerism: the Edsel. Even though not all the returns are in, this looks like the biggest bomb since Hiroshima. Something obviously went drastically wrong, and the bottom-line impact of another Edsel may place Ford in financial jeopardy. On the other hand, the country is clearly in the midst of boom times—you simply can't sit back and watch GM and Chrysler climb all over you. Should you recommend that Ford

A. **conduct a market survey to find out what the American public doesn't like about the Edsel and then redesign it to take advantage of the results of this survey?**

B. **conduct a study to find out which of their assumptions about the Edsel were wrong and resulted in the production of a car that, despite their best efforts, the American public wouldn't buy?**

C. **discontinue production of new models and go back to the models that they already know the public will buy?**

SOLUTIONS: *The '57 Lemon*

A. **You recommend that Ford conduct a market survey to find out what the American public doesn't like about the Edsel; then redesign it to take advantage of the results of this survey. −1 point.** Information can help you make better decisions, providing that the cost of the information does not exceed the gain produced by that information and that the information you are seeking is the *right* information. You have produced a sow's ear, and conducting a survey to obtain information about how to turn it into a silk purse could result in your throwing even more money away.

B. **You recommend that Ford conduct a study to find out which of their assumptions about the Edsel were wrong and resulted in the production of a car that, despite their best efforts, the American public wouldn't buy. 5 points.** You acted in accordance with what you thought was the best information available. It wasn't. You had better find out why this wasn't the best information available, otherwise how can you ever have faith in basing decisions on information you have acquired? Adopting this action is not only critical for this decision, but for future decisions as well.

C. **You convince Ford to discontinue production of new models and go back to the models that you already know the public will buy. 2 points.** This action will certainly improve your near-term payoffs. However, it will not favorably impact your decision-making structure, and failure to repair the flaws in this structure may result in other disasters down the road. *When making decisions, it pays to think about other related decisions that might occur—one swallow doth not a summer make.*

WHAT ACTUALLY HAPPENED

Ford conducted the study suggested in alternative B and discovered that the American buying public was segmented according to lifestyle. This discovery resulted in spectacular successes: the Thunderbird and the Mustang.

Much of Detroit's current malaise stems from its inability to work with information. After the oil crisis of the 1970s, Detroit inaugurated a program to build more fuel-efficient vehicles. When the boom times came in the 1990s, Detroit focused much of its attention on the production of sports utility vehicles (SUVs)—gas guzzlers with high profit margins. Cadillac is now trying to off-load its Escalades on China.

The auto industry has a history of ignoring valuable information. Even though Ford came up with winners in the Mustang and Thunderbird, it fought the public interest tooth and nail on safety, environmental, and social issues, which were clearly of considerable concern. It opposed seat belt and air bag legislation, opposed fuel economy (as noted above) and the Clean Air Act, and resisted alternative-fuel vehicles. Whether the government will continue to bail out the auto industry—and how it will react if that happens—is still to be determined, but if that does take place, they would be well advised to make better use of information than they have in the past.

Wake-Up Call

Two days ago, something happened—and you knew it wasn't good. You felt a severe pain in your upper chest and became short of breath. These are classic symptoms of a heart attack, and when you took a good look at yourself, you realized you were a prime candidate—considerably overweight, sedentary lifestyle, lots of stress. A quick visit to a cardiologist ensued, and he told you your arteries were badly blocked. This could happen again, and the next time you might not be so lucky. It's a wake-up call, but how do you answer the bell? Your cardiologist informs you that three alternatives are open to you, and you have to decide which is right for you.

A. **Drugs and diet.** You can take drugs that will dissolve the cholesterol buildup and change your diet to reduce your cholesterol level in the future.

B. **Angioplasty.** This is a procedure that involves cleaning out the arteries, either by balloon, laser, or mechanical device. You'll be in the hospital for a day or so.

C. **Bypass surgery.** New routes for blood flow to the heart are surgically created to replace those that are blocked. You'll be in the hospital for a few days.

SOLUTIONS: *Wake-Up Call*

A. **Drugs and diet. −3 points.** This is a time when you had better sit back and take action, as you won't have the opportunity to make any more decisions if you end up dead. Drugs and diet are just too slow in a situation in which you simply cannot take the risk of another heart attack. You would choose this option if you had not had a heart attack and your cardiologist hadn't informed you that you needed to reduce your cholesterol.

B. **Angioplasty. 5 points.** After eliminating alternative A as a possibility, you have to decide which of the other two to choose. There is a strong inference you should heed—if your cardiologist had felt that the situation required urgent measures, you'd be undergoing bypass surgery right now. *An important part of obtaining full value from information is to use the negative inferences available from information that has not been given to you—Sherlock Holmes's dog that didn't bark in the night.*

C. **Bypass surgery. 2 points.** This is certainly better than alternative A, but surgery is riskier than nonsurgical procedures, and there are some nasty bugs floating around hospitals, so the less time you spend there, the better. As mentioned before, if this were unquestionably the best option, your cardiologist would have taken the matter out of your hands.

It's worth noting that this scenario involves other aspects of information that are not discussed here. To have made this decision effectively, you needed to know that one has to act quickly when one has warning signs of a heart attack. You needed to know that nonsurgical procedures are less risky than surgery. You needed to know that hospitals can be reservoirs of infectious diseases. Although there is such a thing as information overload, more information is generally better than less information—and information from informed sources is better than information from uninformed sources. A great source of information for situations such as this is patient support groups, where you can talk to individuals who have encountered situations similar to the ones that you are encountering. They are knowledgeable and sympathetic—otherwise they wouldn't be part of a patient support group. One of the best things about the Internet is that it makes an incredible amount of information available. If you have a decision to make, it's a great source of relevant—and irrelevant—information.

The One

After two and a half years, there is very little doubt in your mind that Michelle could be the one. For the most part, it's been a dream relationship—you enjoy many of the same activities, and you have been there for each other when it counted. You took a one-week vacation together in Florida to test the waters, and things couldn't have gone better. Michelle obviously thinks so, too. You're not the most intuitive guy in the world, but you realize that questions such as "How many children do you think are ideal?" are probably not rhetorical. However, you recently read an article that summed up your view perfectly; it said that most guys aren't afraid of getting married, they're afraid of getting into a bad marriage. It might be time to fish or cut bait. Should you

A. **propose that the two of you live together to see how things work out?**

B. **take the plunge and show up with a ring?**

C. **wait for her to bring up the subject of marriage in no uncertain terms?**

SOLUTIONS: *The One*

A. **You propose that the two of you live together to see how things work out. 5 points.** Let's face it, what you really want is a guarantee that you won't be trapping yourself in a bad marriage. This is the best way of really getting to know someone; if there are potential problems, you'll find out about it before you are in too deep. By proposing this step, you will be making it clear that you have an interest in a deeper relationship; if she reacts adversely to this, you'll also obtain more information—such as how she reacts when she doesn't immediately get her way. *There is almost always a price associated with acquiring information, but probably more bad decisions have been made by people unwilling to pay for information than by those who paid too much for information.*

B. You take the plunge and show up with a ring. 4 points. A very, very, very solid second choice. If there are obvious reasons why suggesting that you live together is not a possible alternative, this option moves to the fore-front. She knows you're Mr. Right, and you're pretty sure about her as well. Almost certainly many couples have embarked on happy marriages from a less solid foundation than the two of you now enjoy. If it weren't for your cold feet, this would probably be a slam dunk.

C. You wait for her to bring up the subject of marriage in no uncertain terms. −2 points. She thinks she's already done that. The ball is clearly in your court, and when it's your move in a game, you can't just pass up the turn. You obviously see major payoffs from a happy marriage, and even though waiting for another hint may buy you a little time, you won't learn anything you don't know already, and you will put doubt in Michelle's mind that you're Mr. Right.

As with all commodities, there is a point when the returns associated with the acquisition of information start to diminish—and may even start to hamper a successful decision. The classic example from economics is the acquisition of bottled water in the desert. The first few bottles of water may save your life—but there comes a point at which you simply don't need any more water to make your way out of the desert, and beyond that is the point where the extra water takes the place of supplies that are more urgently needed. In the marriage scenario, you've just about reached the point of diminishing returns as far as information is concerned.

One can actually see the results of additional information in the typical stories of couples who get married. Those who rush to the altar too early in the game often do not have sufficient information on which to base such a critical decision as marriage. Those who spend time learning about each other are better positioned to know whether the marriage will work. Finally, those who spend too much time acquiring information may find that the moment has passed them by or that the other party decides that things have gone on too long and looks elsewhere. There's no ironclad rule, but there comes a time when you simply have to either fish or cut bait.

Major Decision

Your hands were shaking when you opened that letter from Stanford, but it was good news—a spot is waiting for you in the upcoming freshman class! Four years of hard work in high school, with your family pulling for you all the way, had finally paid off. Unfortunately, after a brief honeymoon, they're no longer pulling for you, but at you. Dad thinks you should major in business or engineering, something with a bottom-line payoff and a guaranteed job when you graduate. Mom, on the other hand, thinks that it would be nice to have a doctor or a lawyer in the family and points out that even though you would have to spend an additional three to five years in school *after* college, doctors and lawyers can easily pull down six-figure salaries. While there is certainly merit in each plan, it seems like they're trying to project their values on to you, when you don't even know what your values are. Meanwhile, you have to select your classes for the fall semester, and this selection depends upon what your major will be. Should you

A. take Dad's advice and major in something like engineering or business, with a good job waiting when you graduate?
B. listen to Mom and go for a pre-med or a pre-law degree, thus planning to continue your education after college?
C. refuse to declare a major and take a wide selection of courses to fulfill Stanford's breadth requirements?

SOLUTIONS: *Major Decision*

A. **You take Dad's advice and major in something like engineering or business, with a good job waiting when you graduate. 2 points.** This is a slightly curious situation; your payoffs for this decision consist of determining exactly what your long-term payoffs are! Do you really want to be an engineer or go into business? If you know you do, you can choose this option comfortably, but that doesn't seem to be the case here. *Committing yourself to a course of action won't help you determine what your payoffs are; don't leap before you look—or before you evaluate your payoffs.*

B. **You listen to Mom and go for a pre-med or a pre-law degree, thus planning to continue your education after college. 1 point.** Once again, there's absolutely nothing wrong with being a doctor or a lawyer, if it's what you want. If it's what you don't want, you are committing a large part of your life to study what you don't enjoy studying and to do what you won't like doing. This alternative is poorer than the previous alternative because you are committing yourself for a longer period of time.

C. You refuse to declare a major and take a wide selection of courses to fulfill Stanford's breadth requirements. 5 points. Sometimes there is a cost associated with acquiring valuable information, but here it's totally free. You are going to have to take a lot of these courses anyway; so why not do it now and find out more about what *your* long-term payoffs really are?

It may seem somewhat deceptive to have presented this quiz after mentioning that there comes a time when you have to make a decision—but there will come a time when the decision presented here *must* be made. There's nothing wrong with postponing a decision that has to be made in order to acquire information that will help you make that decision as long as by doing so you are improving your Bayes' Criterion payoffs from making the decision. This scenario stands in contrast to the marriage scenario presented earlier in this chapter, in which your payoffs for making a decision will start to decrease at a certain point and may actually disappear if you don't make the decision. Part of the difficulty there is that there is no formally announced deadline for actually making the marriage decision. Here there is such a deadline—at some stage you will actually have to declare a major, as no one has ever graduated from a university with a degree in randomly taken courses. However, every bit of information you can accumulate until that deadline will almost certainly help you make the correct decision when the deadline actually arrives.

Hostile Takeover

One of the perks you enjoy as the head of the R & D division of your company is the annual golfing outing with the head honchos—nice course, good food, and drinks flowing freely at the nineteenth hole. Just as you were lining up your five-foot putt for a par, the vice president of the company, one of your foursome, starts talking about a takeover bid that is coming from a huge manufacturing corporation, one with a reputation for chewing up small companies—and their employees. You step back from the putt, take a deep breath, and drain it like Tiger at the Masters—despite the fact that the VP obviously assumes you knew about this when this was the first you'd heard about it. As you head to the next hole, a par three, you're thinking about an ace you have yet to play—not on the par three but on an exciting development in your division that could revolutionize the water-desalinization industry. You don't ordinarily have access to the VP except through a series of chain-of-command e-mails and interviews, and you've basically only got the back nine and the party afterward to talk to him—if that's the right move. Should you

- A. inform the VP of the breakthrough in water desalinization in the hopes that it will stiffen the executive's resolve to resist the takeover?
- B. keep quiet and discuss this development with members of your division, to get their take and their feeling about which course to pursue?
- C. tell the VP that you don't think their corporate culture will mesh well with yours?

SOLUTIONS: *Hostile Takeover*

A. **You inform the VP of the breakthrough in water desalinization in the hopes that it will stiffen the executive's resolve to resist the takeover.**
   −3 points. It would be hard to come up with a worse plan. First of all, the VP is obviously a blabbermouth, and it's dollars to doughnuts you're giving away your hole card. Also, the possession of this technology may make the big manufacturer even more eager to acquire you.

B. **You keep quiet and discuss this development with members of your division, to get their take and feeling about which course to pursue. 5 points.**
   This must be the best move. You want to take advantage of the fact that you know something the executives don't so that you can plan the best way to deal with anticipated developments. Don't give anything away here—you have information now that is valuable to you, and you don't want to give them information that may be equally valuable to them. *Even more valuable than knowledge is knowing in addition that your opponent does not possess that knowledge.*

C. **You tell the VP that you don't think their corporate culture will mesh well with yours. 1 point.**
   This isn't as bad as alternative A, and it may cause the VP to reconsider his position on the upcoming takeover. Or not—maybe there are a lot of incentives for the higher-ups to acquiesce. You simply cannot gauge his reaction, but at least you're not giving the show away. This is definitely one of those times when loose lips sink ships.

There's another reason it's a good idea to take this information back to the division and let them chew on it. Even though you're an executive, as head of the R & D division, you do not have the responsibility nor the power to make policy decisions such as this one. Mistakes in assessing a situation are often forgiven, but mistakes in knowing your place in the chain of command are much more likely to be fatal. A classic case in point, at a very high level, occurred in 1981 after President Reagan had been shot. While Reagan was in the hospital, General Alexander Haig, who was serving as secretary of state, announced at a national news conference that "I'm in charge here." Very good general— but weak on the Constitution of the United States. The line of succession on the death or incapacitation of a president puts the secretary of state behind the vice president (every school child knows that), the speaker of the House (many people know that), and the president pro tempore of the Senate (probably only wonks know that—I didn't). Haig resigned as secretary of state in 1982—he wasn't fired for his gaffe, but one has to believe that his influence and credibility diminished drastically after that incident. Haig, like many others, undoubtedly had good reason to regret the result of a decision made without the use of readily available knowledge.

On that note, and because the use of information is such an important topic, here's one more quiz to top off the chapter.

Well Heeled

Even though there's no current Imelda Marcos—owner of over a thousand pairs of expensive shoes—on the scene, your upscale shoe business is doing quite well. It seems that there are more than enough wealthy women—or their husbands—willing to pay you, Manolo Blahnik, and Jimmy Choo upward of five hundred bucks for a pair of shoes that to the naked eye seem to consist of $20 worth of leather, $20 worth of workmanship, and $460 or more worth of label. Your bottom line is extraordinarily healthy—with a profit margin like that, how could it not be?—and you're looking for possible areas in which to expand. Which area do you think offers the most opportunity to add to your already substantial bottom line?

A. Medium-priced shoes, to take advantage of the fact that every woman wants to own at least one pricey item of clothing

B. Salons in cities other than Paris, London, New York, and Beverly Hills (where your stores are currently located), to put your shoes within easy reach of those women who prefer a personalized shopping experience to online shopping

C. Upscale accessories, such as handbags, to accompany your upscale shoes

SOLUTIONS: *Well Heeled*

A. You decide to offer medium-priced shoes to take advantage of the fact that every woman wants to own at least one pricey item of clothing. −2 points. The potential market may be much larger than the one you currently reach, but there's no guarantee that you will penetrate it. What can be guaranteed, though, is that in attempting to do so, you will no longer enjoy the cachet that comes with a brand name associated with pricey exclusivity. You don't see Rolex offering cheap watches or even medium-priced ones. They sell luxury watches. Yes, Mercedes has a C class, but it's out of reach of the Toyota crowd. Don't even think about doing this. *Abandoning a brand identity is the same type of mistake that a football team that has run the ball successfully down to the two-yard line makes when it throws a pass that is intercepted—a creative solution is only required when your bread-and-butter approach is failing.*

B. **You decide to open salons in cities other than Paris, London, New York, and Beverly Hills (where your stores are currently located) to put your shoes within easy reach of those women who prefer a personalized shopping experienced to online shopping. 0 points.** Exactly how is this going to help you? You're not going to locate to Pittsburgh, and if you rent space on Michigan Avenue in Chicago or the Via Veneto in Rome, it's going to cost you a fortune—and may not materially increase your sales. Take advantage of information; everyone knows the world is moving to the convenience of online shopping. True, the individual stores are very likely to show a profit, but it's not the best use of your capital.

C. **You decide to offer upscale accessories, such as handbags, to accompany your upscale shoes. 5 points.** Almost certainly the winning move. You can create matched sets using virtually the same materials and work-manship. You can keep your reputation for upscale quality. True, you do have competition in this area—but you also have a great deal of potential for profit. It's not a sure thing, but it's a lot better than the other alternatives, and it was the one adopted by Manolo Blahnik and Jimmy Choo, both of whom expanded their successful lines of expensive shoes by adding upscale accoutrements.

We live in an era in which we are deluged with information. Much of it is irrelevant, but you simply cannot afford to ignore developments that impact important areas of your life. Whether that area is personal or business, it's critical to maintain current information about what's happening now that's relevant to you.

CHAPTER 11 # The Balance of Power

ame theory, probably the most famous branch of decision theory, is the study of decisions involving strategic interactions with other parties. In the following example, we can see this at work in business. Businesses often succeed or fail depending upon how well they can outwit their rivals.

Fat Chance

Everyone wants to be healthy, wealthy, and wise—or at least the first two, since a lot of people seem to assume they're already wise, but it's hard to perform major self-deception on the issues of health and wealth. As CEO of Healthy Humans, you're in the business of manufacturing health food. In looking over your product lines, you've noticed that you don't do so well when going up against high-profile rivals with celebrity spokespeople;

you seem to do better when you have the field to yourself. However, the overall balance sheet is healthy, and you're looking for new products to add to your line. Should you go with

A. a flavor-enhanced dried vegetable snack designed to be a substitute for potato chips and other variations of junk food? It's competitive with potato chips in taste tests.

B. an energy drink that is all the rage in Japan because it not only energizes you but curbs your appetite? You have an opportunity for an exclusive American franchise.

C. a toothpaste from Scandinavia that seems not only to leave your teeth whiter and your breath fresher but also to lower your cholesterol?

SOLUTIONS: *Fat Chance*

A. You decide to offer a flavor-enhanced dried vegetable snack designed to be a substitute for potato chips and other variations of junk food. 1 point.
On the plus side, this could be a huge hit—if you can find a market for it. But where is that market to come from? There are lots of competitors making trail mix, protein bars, and all sorts of healthy snack alternatives to flavor-enhanced dried vegetables. Even if they don't have celebrity spokespeople, they are well known to the snack-food-buying public—you've seen them countless times in the supermarket. There are too many competitors.

B. You concentrate your energies on an energy drink that is all the rage in Japan because it not only energizes you but curbs your appetite. −2 points.

You may not be able to name your competitors in the healthy snack food department, but you sure can in the energy drink market. Gatorade. Red Bull. Don't get sucked in by the exclusive franchise bait—you're going to have to work awfully hard to find a place on the shelves.

C. **You decide to stock a toothpaste from Scandinavia that seems to not only leave your teeth whiter and your breath fresher but your cholesterol lower. 5 points.** Wow! Here's something that could be unique. The easiest way to win a game is to be the only one to show up. Come up with a catchy brand name and you may very well have a humongous hit on your hands that no one will be able to match. *Finding a niche market is a move from game theory (and the art of war); when you can't conquer an opponent with a frontal attack, try for a flanking move.*

Twentieth-Century Foxiness

Mathematicians had spent most of their efforts prior to the Middle Ages measuring and counting things. Much of the mathematics of the seventeenth, eighteenth, and nineteenth centuries was devoted to its applications in sciences and engineering, but the twentieth century marked the breakout of mathematics into the social sciences.

The seminal book in this area was *Theory of Games and Economic Behavior*, written by the mathematician John von Neumann and the economist Oskar Morgenstern. The coming of World War II aroused new interest in game theory, as it turned out to be especially useful for analyzing many different types of military conflict situations. For an entertaining and easy-to-read treatment of the subject, J. D. Williams's *The Compleat Strategyst*, published more than half a century ago by the Rand Corporation (one of the early heavy users of game theory), remains a classic.

Not all games end in victory or defeat. In many instances, the other party may be colleague or competitor, friend or foe, but often the relationship reaches a point where a balance of power of some sort has been reached. This balance of power is referred to as an *equilibrium solution*. Equilibrium solutions are common features of all sorts of interactions. The equilibrium may be robust, in the sense that it can survive significant disturbances. A marble in a soup bowl is a good example: a minor disturbance will cause the marble to move, but it will eventually resettle at the bottom of the bowl. It takes a really severe jolt to shake the marble out of the bowl. Alternatively, an equilibrium can be very delicate: if one were to balance that marble on the flat blade of a knife (it's almost impossible to balance it on the knife's edge), the slightest disturbance would be enough to cause the marble to roll off the knife.

The equilibrium solution may be desirable or undesirable, and each of the parties to the equilibrium solution may view the

By the Numbers

A terrific example of an equilibrium situation can be seen when Rafael Nadal, the present number-one-ranked player in tennis, serves to Roger Federer, the former number-one-ranked player. Nadal has the choice of serving to Federer's cannon-like forehand or his not-quite-so-strong backhand. Federer can position himself to anticipate a serve to his forehand or backhand. The following table gives Nadal's success percentages in winning the point when he is serving to Federer.

	FEDERER ANTICIPATES	
NADAL SERVES	TO HIS FOREHAND	TO HIS BACKHAND
To Federer's Forehand	50	40
To Federer's Backhand	70	60

Nadal invariably serves to Federer's backhand, and Federer always anticipates this—an equilibrium position. Suppose that Nadal serves instead to Federer's forehand. Even though Federer still anticipates a serve to his backhand, Nadal's success percentage declines from 60 to 40. Similarly, suppose that Federer anticipates a serve to his forehand and Nadal continues to serve to his backhand. Federer's success percentage decreases from 40 ($=100 - 60$) to 30 ($=100 - 70$).

This is the signature of an equilibrium position—the first person to depart from his equilibrium strategy shows a loss by doing so.

At any rate, as we shall see in this chapter, equilibrium solutions occur in diverse environments and offer wide scope for improving one's decision-making abilities.

solution differently. Such is often the case when peace is achieved between two warring parties; both sides may genuinely desire to maintain the peace, or one (or both) sides may view peace as an opportunity to regroup in order to pursue further hostilities.

Magic Moments

Things were a little rocky about a year ago, but the last few months of your marriage have been practically everything you've hoped they would be, and the primary reason seems to be that your husband has been practically everything you've hoped he would be. He has been a devoted father and an affectionate and loving husband. You've never been one to look gift horses in the mouth, but it has accidentally come to your attention that your husband's exemplary behavior during the past few months may have arisen out of guilt: he had been having an affair with a woman in his office. According to the best information available, it is now a thing of the past, and he has stayed on the straight and narrow ever since. You're more than just a little hurt, and you're trying to decide which of the following ways to react.

A. **Do your best to forget about it, realizing that this may be one of those times when silence is golden.**

B. **Let him know that you know but play the part of the forgiving wife.**

C. **Let him know that you know and use this knowledge to get some concessions.**

SOLUTIONS: *Magic Moments*

A. **You do your best to forget about it, realizing that this may be one of those times when silence is golden. 5 points.** A stable and happy marriage is a classic example of an equilibrium solution, and at the moment, that's precisely what you've got. It is up to you to make sure that the information you have just acquired does *not* affect the payoffs of both players so that the equilibrium solution is still seen as optimal by both participants.

B. **You let him know that you know but play the part of the forgiving wife. 0 points.** As soon as you let the cat out of the bag, you are potentially altering the payoffs. An equilibrium solution can have varying degrees of stability. Although this particular equilibrium solution may not be affected by minor changes in the payoffs, you have no guarantee that the resultant changes in the payoffs will be so small that the equilibrium solution will still hold.

C. **You let him know that you know and use this knowledge to get some concessions. −2 points.** This action is most likely to generate major changes in the payoffs, with the result that the equilibrium solution will no longer be applicable. *While equilibrium solutions will often survive minor alterations in payoffs and actions, major modifications to the payoffs will often entirely change the nature of the game.*

One frequently hears the term "win-win solution." Equilibrium solutions can be excellent examples of these, and they can occur in a diverse array of situations. Personal relationships, especially friendships that have developed over a long period, exhibit the full range of stability with regard to equilibrium solutions. Many of us have developed friendships with people who are extremely sensitive; criticism of any sort, or even inattention, threatens to destroy the equilibrium. The other side of the coin is the friendship that is so strong it can withstand almost any adverse event. There are examples of good friends who remain good friends even as each undergoes a divorce and remarriage—to the friend's spouse!

Equilibrium states are not just the result of an uneasy détente between rivals, as the next quiz demonstrates.

The Crash

Your husband has always been a great driver, and you've always felt comfortable when he took the wheel for either a trip to the grocery store or a long expedition. However, a ten-year record of perfect safety just came to an end when he failed to look both ways and plowed into a car that had just finished making a turn. The damage to both vehicles appeared to be relatively minor, but he was undoubtedly responsible for the accident, and the driver of the other vehicle has hired a lawyer and is suing for compensation for injuries. Your car will take a week or so to be repaired, and in the meantime, your husband has points on his driver's license and has to kiss the "good driver" insurance discount goodbye. When the two of you went to visit some friends last evening, he uncharacter-istically asked you to drive, and he is clearly reluctant to get behind the wheel. Nonetheless, he's going to have to do so— when you live in Los Angeles, you've got to drive. Should you

A. **let him choose when he wants to start driving again?**
B. **hand him the keys the next time you get back in the car as if nothing has happened?**
C. **suggest that he enroll in a course in safe driving?**

SOLUTIONS: *The Crash*

A. **You decide to be patient and let him choose when he wants to start driving again. 5 points.** Normal, confident driving is an equilibrium state—and your husband has been knocked out of that state. He needs to reestablish the original equilibrium, and this is best accomplished by letting him drift back to that position at a pace that is comfortable for him.

B. **You hand him the keys the next time you get back in the car as if nothing has happened. 2 points.** While you are displaying confidence in him, you are also acting as if the original equilibrium had not been disturbed. You both know it has, and if you try to force a system back to its original equilibrium, it might cause an overreaction— in this case, your husband might drive too cautiously.

C. **You suggest that he enroll in a course in safe driving. −1 point.** When a dog makes a mess on the carpet, one training technique is to rub its nose in it. Bad dog! However, your husband—unlike the dog—knows better. *The important point is to restore the system to its original comfortable equilibrium—not establish a new and different equilibrium.* If your husband were a habitually dangerous driver, the accident could serve as a wake-up call, and you would want to reestablish a new and different equilibrium. That's not the case here.

As the previous scenario shows, an equilibrium solution is not something that is set in stone. Equilibria can be disturbed, and new equilibria obtained. A classic example occurs when there are two or three companies selling a similar product and market share has reached a relatively stable configuration. If one company decides to cut its prices in a bid to increase its market share, it is quite likely to trigger a round of price-cutting by the other companies. The net result is that market share will probably not change by much, but all companies will find their profitability reduced. Such was the situation in a relatively common occurrence in the 1940s and 1950s. Two gas stations at the same intersection would engage in a price war—one would even see signs at the stations announcing that they were engaged in a "gas war." Sadly for contemporary consumers, this was before OPEC—back when prices were in the range of 25 cents per gallon. It is unlikely that those days will come again.

Equilibrium solutions can arise in a variety of situations, some of which involve agents with competing interests and some of which don't. In those situations where there are agents with competing interests, one must try to anticipate how they will react to an equilibrium-disturbing action. Accurately predicting this reaction, and the consequent effect on relevant payoffs, is an important part of determining the correct decision. Remember the quote attributed to the physicist Niels Bohr—"Prediction is difficult, especially of the future"—and Bohr was only talking about nuclear physics! Making predictions of how agents with competing interest would react is every bit as difficult.

People Who Need People

F ar be it from me to contradict Barbra Streisand, but people who need people might *not* be the luckiest people in the world. There are all sorts of reasons that people need other people or that organizations need other organizations. This chapter looks at decisions involving coalitions and cooperative solutions to game situations.

Housing Development

The surge in gated communities has been extremely good for your business, and it looks like things are about to get even better. You run a house-painting business specializing in McMansions, and a developer has recently announced plans for a colony of about fifty of these. They're going to be located on a lake, and the community is also going to have a golf course designed by Tiger Woods. The people who buy these houses don't even bother to haggle; if they like the house, they write the check. You feel your chances of landing the house-painting contract are pretty good, but they'll be even better if you can offer the developer a package deal. Time is of the essence here: you only have enough of it to begin negotiations with one or two groups. Should you try to ally with

A. **home-security specialists, using the slogan "We protect both the inside and outside of your home"?**

B. **landscapers, to create a coordinated pleasing exterior for the houses?**

C. **interior designers, with whom you can ally to purchase supplies such as paint more cheaply?**

SOLUTIONS: *Housing Development*

A. **You ally with home-security specialists using the slogan "We protect both the inside and outside of your home." −1 point.** Other than the slogan, neither party has anything to offer the other. They don't do anything in common, they have no shared contacts or industry connections, and they don't hire the same type of workers. The parties here can benefit from each other roughly as much as a fish can benefit from a bicycle. *Forming the right coalition is even more important than just forming a coalition. The wrong coalition may actually be counterproductive to the interests of the individual entities comprising it.*

B. **You decide to partner with landscapers to create a coordinated pleasing exterior for the houses. 5 points.** It's a natural fit. Although you have no direct shared economic benefits, you have shared aesthetic ones and can work together to produce a pleasing result. At this level, homes are viewed as works of art, and making sure that the exterior aspects do not clash is an enticing prospect for the developer.

C. **Interior designers, with whom you can ally to purchase supplies such as paint more cheaply. 0 points.** In fact, there is a real danger here—the developer is likely to want to hire specific interior designers, and if you choose the wrong partner, you're almost certainly going to find yourself on the outside looking in. Let's face it, what generally gets a house written up in *Better Homes and Gardens* is its inside, not its outside—and you're responsible for the outside. Absolutely nobody is worrying about the cost of paint in enterprises such as this, and any cost reductions that might be obtained will only have a marginal impact on the bottom line.

Returning for a moment to Barbra Streisand's signature song, there are two questions that must be answered in deciding whether you belong to the nation of people who need people. The first is: do you *really* need people? In forming a coalition, compromises invariably have to be made, and you must be sure that the increase in payoffs accruing to the coalition (and what is more important, your share of those payoffs) will be worth the compromises you will have to make. Many successful projects would be derailed by a coalition; there really are situations in which too many cooks spoil the broth. In the house-painting scenario, you can be almost certain that a coalition of more than two parties would doom any chance of success because having too many parties involved will reduce the developer's options when it comes to making creative decisions.

Chemistry is the study of how simple substances combine to make useful, more complicated substances. It is not surprising that chemistry is cited as an important factor in a good coalition—whether that coalition is Romeo and Juliet or Procter and Gamble. But coalitions can be just as important in creating good chemistry, as the following scenario demonstrates.

Long Chain

As one of the directors of the DuPont Corporation, you've been a strong advocate of research designed to produce new chemical products, and it seems to have paid off big-time. In 1935 Wallace Carothers, one of the "better living through chemistry" boys in the lab, has produced a synthetic fiber by manipulating long-chain hydrocarbons. This new stuff, which you've trade named "Nylon," seems to have a variety of uses—from manufacturing synthetic substitutes for rubber in automobile tires to substitutes for silk stockings. You just brought out Nylon stockings in 1940, and they have been a huge commercial hit. Now you have to make a decision about how to supply Nylon, on which you have the patent. Should you

- **A. remain the sole supplier of Nylon until the patent runs out, guaranteeing that you and only you will produce Nylon stockings?**
- **B. wait until the sales from Nylon products repay the cost of development and then license production of Nylon to other users?**
- **C. expand the market for Nylon by immediately licensing its production?**

SOLUTIONS: *Long Chain*

A. You remain the sole supplier of Nylon until the patent runs out, guaranteeing that you and only you will produce Nylon stockings. 2 points. It's certainly tempting. However, you can bet the farm that even as you are counting your profits from Nylon products, others are looking at ways to execute an end run around the restrictions of the patent. Wallace Carothers isn't the only good chemist; you've got to look for a way to minimize actions of potential rivals.

B. You wait until the profits from Nylon products repay the cost of development and then license production of Nylon to other users. 4 points. Having decided to let others in on the action, the only question is how soon to do so. However, there are two downsides to this particular option. The first has been mentioned in the analysis of the sole-supplier option. The second is that the sooner you let others in on the action, the sooner they may find new and enticing uses for Nylon undreamt of by your people. *In both business and personal relations, you do better by building alliances than by conquest.*

C. You expand the market for Nylon by immediately licensing its production. 5 points. It's hard to see how this can hurt. By cutting others in on the action, you will undoubtedly greatly expand the alternatives for your product; a piece of each pie in a pie factory is a lot more pie than contained in a single pie, no matter how large.

WHAT ACTUALLY HAPPENED

DuPont waited until the profits from Nylon products repaid the cost of development and then licensed other suppliers.

> It worked out well—but it could conceivably have backfired, even though a backfire would have been a low-probabiity event, given the quick success of Nylon as a commercial product.

Coalitions come in many different types and many different strengths—from "'til death do us part" to "adversity makes strange bedfellows." While it is certainly true that often the weak will seek coalitions in order to strengthen their positions, the strong (as in the Nylon scenario) will seek coalitions in order to maximize the advantage of their strength.

Normally, a coalition is formed by mutual agreement, although coalitions can be forced on the unwilling. (One of the great euphemisims ever employed for such a forced coalition was the Greater East Asia Co-Prosperity Sphere, an alliance forced upon weaker nations by Japan during the run-up to World War II.) Of course, many of the principles that have already been studied for making decisions—minimax, the Bayes' Criterion, etc.—will apply to determine whether a coalition is a good idea, but each party may have a different criterion to apply. A strong company can often acquire a failing one to make use of some aspect of the acquired company's business—the strong company uses the Bayes' Criterion to improve its long-term payoffs, whereas the acquired company seeks the support of the strong company in order to survive.

Once you decide that it is in your interest to form a coalition, you may still face a critical decision: which coalition to form. The choice made in the final scenario in this chapter shaped much of the history of the twentieth century.

The Man of Steel

Nobody could remember or pronounce your name, so you changed it to Joseph Stalin, the man of steel. It's been an accurate name, for even though you possessed no formal military training, you were able to defend the Russian Revolution against attacks from both within and without during those first critical years after 1917. Now, however, there's another crisis. This time, it's personal. Lenin has just died and has named Leon Trotsky as his heir apparent. Lenin even went so far, in his political testament, to recommend that you be removed from your post as secretary general, but you successfully managed to suppress that document. Your goal is to become the next leader of Russia and consolidate the gains of the revolution, but Trotsky still harbors these visionary dreams of leading a worldwide uprising against the bourgeoisie. You are number two behind Trotsky in the struggle for power, and there are two others, Lev Kamenev and Grigori Zinoviev, who can still play a role in the power struggle. There is almost certainly a route to leadership here, but one misstep and you are liable to be pushing up daisies—they play for keeps in this league. No matter what your plan, you will have to execute it smoothly. Is your best bet

A. to look for a way to eliminate Trotsky first and then remove the little fish?
B. to form a coalition with Kamenev and Zinoviev to get rid of Trotsky and then make your play for the starring role?
C. to form an alliance with Trotsky to dispose of Kamenev and Zinoviev and then wait for Trotsky to make a mistake?

SOLUTIONS: *The Man of Steel*

A. You decide to look for a way to eliminate Trotsky first and then remove the little fish. —1 point. There is a double danger here. First, as things stand, Trotsky is stronger than you are, so he would be the favorite in a head-to-head encounter. Even if you got past the first obstacle, there is a reasonable chance that Kamenev and Zinoviev might realize you can't be trusted and band together. If they enlist help from the Trotskyites, you are whatever the Russian word is for "toast."

B. You form a coalition with Kamenev and Zinoviev to get rid of Trotsky and then make your play for the starring role. 5 points. This is clearly your best strategy, as it certainly gives you your best chance at eliminating Trotsky from the field. When the dust has settled, you will be the clear favorite to emerge in the top spot. *A coalition is often most likely to be profitable if the strength of the coalition is sufficiently great to force a realignment of the existing power structure.* That seems to be the case here.

C. You form an alliance with Trotsky to dispose of Kamenev and Zinoviev and then wait for Trotsky to make a mistake. —2 points. There are many flaws in this action. There is not as much incentive for Trotsky to form such an alliance because he is already top dog. Even if he does, he will still be stronger than you, and he will be on the alert. As a matter of fact, he may well take steps to eliminate you, figuring that it is wise to do unto others before others do unto him.

WHAT ACTUALLY HAPPENED

Stalin has been called oppressive, brutal, and paranoid, but no one ever called him stupid. A master at behind-the-scenes maneuvers, he first formed a three-man "troika" with Kamenev and Zinoviev to get rid of Trotsky and then consolidated his stranglehold on power by eliminating the two of them. In game theory terms, he first maximized the cooperative gains and then maximized his share of them. Stalin then conducted massive purges of his opponents during the 1930s. No more Mr. Nice Guy.

What You Can Learn from History

Heads of organizations are almost never the brilliant loners. The world is filled with individuals whose social skills and ability to network are considerably greater than their raw talent for succeeding at the job—yet often the networkers are the ones who get promoted. That's because many organizations are teams, and getting the most out of colleagues is often just as important as getting the job done yourself.

This may be the first sentence ever published in which the names of J. Robert Oppenheimer and Magic Johnson are juxtaposed—but it is appropriate, because both were unquestioned masters of getting the most out of their colleagues. Michael Jordan may have been Magic Johnson's superior in scoring and defense, but nobody ever managed to get their teammates to play better basketball than Magic. Similarly, Oppenheimer never won a Nobel Prize, but it would be difficult to find a better example of a leader who managed to get an assemblage of immensely talented individuals to function together as a team.

CHAPTER 13 Hurts So Good

When I was younger, I was an avid bridge player. Not only did I enjoy the game, tournament bridge brought together a very colorful collection of characters. One such player was Bob Hamman, many times a world champion and current partner of Bill Gates, a bridge player of lesser ability but somewhat greater repute. The following question was posed to a collection of bridge players, all of whom knew Bob: "You are playing bridge for money in a game with Bob. Which outcome would you prefer— to be a small winner when Bob is a big winner, or to be a small loser when Bob is a big loser?" Overwhelmingly, the respondents voted to take a small financial hit in order to see Bob take a bigger one. Such a situation is known as a *vindictive solution*.

Chip Shot

You're on the cusp of what is going to be a boom industry—producing RFID (radio-frequency identification) chips. These chips have a multitude of uses; they are currently being installed in many passports for secure identification, being used to automatically collect fees for using different forms of transportation, and starting to replace bar codes for product identification. The possibilities are endless, and Colossal Chips has announced that they are producing a chip conforming to industry standards that will retail for $10. This is very good news for you because you can produce the same chip and make a reasonable profit if it retails for $7. Unfortunately, if you decide to do this, there's a chance that Colossal Chips will retail it for $6 simply to eliminate you as a potential threat. The good news is that RFID chips are only a small portion of Colossal's business—they could easily just decide it's not worth the effort. Should you fish, cut bait—or maybe something else? Your options are to

- **A. manufacture the chips.** When Colossal Chips retails them for $10, you'll announce a price of $9. If Colossal goes to $8, you'll go to $7.
- **B. announce that you are planning to manufacture and sell them for $7.**
- **C. try to find manufacturers who produce products that naturally can use or require the chips and bundle your chips with their products.**

SOLUTIONS: *Chip Shot*

A. You go ahead and manufacture the chips. When Colossal Chips retails them for $10, you'll announce

a price of $9. If Colossal goes to $8, you'll go to $7.
−2 points. Sandbagging Colossal Chips is a good way to get your head handed to you. They can afford to take a loss in order to eliminate an annoying rival, and this is a really good way to maximize the annoyance while simultaneously minimizing the probability of your future existence. *A small-stakes player in a high-stakes game always runs the risk that a big player may take a loss in order to inflict a vindictive solution.*

B. **You announce that you are planning to manufacture and sell them for $7. 5 points.** There are times when it is important to withhold information from the enemy—but there are also times when it is important to provide it. This is one of those times. RFIDs are a small portion of Colossal's inventory, and they may decide it is just not worth the effort if you let them see your hole card.

C. **You try to find manufacturers who produce products that naturally can use or require the chips and bundle your chips with their products. 2 points.** This does not pose a direct challenge to Colossal, and so this is likely to be a viable strategy, especially considering that you don't have to expose your price advantage to Colossal. The difficulty here is that you have to do extra work to arrange the liaisons, and your market is limited to those with whom you can make such agreements.

Unlike bridge with Bob, a vindictive solution doesn't necessarily involve taking a jab to the chin just to see a hated rival go down in flames. From the standpoint of Colossal Chips, the vindictive solution of taking a loss can actually be thought of as a Bayes' Criterion strategy—the short-term loss will be offset by the long-term gain of eliminating a potential rival. Vindictive solutions are not just gut reactions. They are often well-planned, strategically motivated decisions to achieve a long-term goal—especially in business.

Vindictive solutions frequently appear in political decisions. One of the most famous historical cases is the following scenario.

The Saturday Night Massacre

It's been less than a year since you, Richard Nixon, were elected to a second term in office, but it looks like the you-know-what is about to hit the fan. The Watergate business seems to get messier and messier. Several months ago, you were forced to authorize Attorney General Elliot Richardson to appoint a special prosecutor to investigate the entire affair, and he came up with Archibald Cox, a Harvard law professor. Cox has been diligent, perhaps too diligent. Last summer the televised hearings revealed that you had secretly installed tape recorders to record your own conversations, including your discussions with your advisors. Cox wants those tapes to use in his investigation. You don't want to let him have the tapes. You want to make sure that you survive this debacle and remain in office. Your advisors have presented three alternatives that they feel are your only choices. Should you

> **A.** turn over the tapes immediately and face the music before the damage gets any worse?
> **B.** fight Cox every inch of the way by whatever legal means available but turn over the tapes once all resources are exhausted?

C. **get the attorney general to fire Cox, even though another special prosecutor will almost certainly have to be appointed?**

SOLUTIONS: *The Saturday Night Massacre*

A. **You turn over the tapes immediately and face the music before the damage gets any worse. 3 points.** Minimax considerations would dictate that this is the best strategy, as making a clean breast of things as soon as possible would doubtless reduce potential adverse consequences. However, this may not be a pure minimax problem.

B. **You fight Cox every inch of the way by whatever legal means available but turn over the tapes once all resources are exhausted. 5 points.** This is probably the best Bayesian solution. Since there is a chance that you may not have to turn over the tapes or can at least delay the inevitable until your term expires, the expected value of this action is significantly greater than the previous one. Simply availing yourself of legal defenses should extend your time in office, and this is probably how you are computing your payoffs. Everyone, even the president, is afforded the protection of the law. *The Bayes' Criterion trumps minimax considerations if there is a significant chance of positive payoffs, as that chance generally outweighs any increase in adverse consequences—at least, in the long run.*

C. **You get the attorney general to fire Cox, even though another special prosecutor will almost certainly have to be appointed. −3 points.** This must be a candidate for one of history's worst possible decisions. The net effect will be to generate a replay of the previous situation, with all payoffs made more unfavorable. The vindictive solution of shooting the bearer of bad tidings may vent a great deal of frustration, but as a rational alternative, it is clearly dominated by the other choices presented here.

WHAT ACTUALLY HAPPENED

Perhaps later historians will be able to discern whether any of the participants used decision theory to analyze the choices confronting Nixon at this crucial juncture. In light of the fact that Nixon actually fired Cox and was later compelled to resign, it doesn't seem that decision theory played an important role in the analysis.

What You Can Learn from History

There are times and places for vindictive solutions, as discussed previously, but because vindictive solutions can backfire big-time, they should be carefully and rationally evaluated before being chosen. The Italian saying that revenge is a dish that is best eaten cold really nails it.

Bitter Fruits

What started with the assassination of Archduke Franz Ferdinand at Sarajevo in 1914 has finally ended more than four years later with the signing of the Armistice Treaty between the Allies and the Central Powers. The Great War, the War to End All Wars, is finally over, and the problem now is to decide what to do with Germany. If it were up to the French, Germany would probably be reduced to a mere province, and their fields would be sown with salt. England is not keen on letting bygones be bygones either. This is the twentieth century, though, and your goal, Woodrow Wilson, is to make sure that this doesn't happen again. In the back of your mind, you remember that the European nations have been fighting wars with one another for more than half a millennium and that you must do your best to break this vicious cycle. You have to steer your way through the Scylla of the demand for retribution by England and France and the Charybdis of an intensely nationalistic Germany. All agree that the German military must disband, but should you also argue for

> **A.** **a version of the *status quo ante*, in which the Germans would pay significant reparations but would lose no territory?**
> **B.** **the death penalty, in which Germany would pay substantial reparations and lose substantial territory?**
> **C.** **a compromise, in which the Germans would pay some reparations and lose some territory?**

SOLUTIONS: *Bitter Fruits*

A. **You argue for a version of the *status quo ante*, in which the Germans would pay significant reparations but would lose no territory. 5 points.** Tradition is that the losers in a war have to pay the price, and so the Germans cannot simply be let off with a slap on the wrist. On the other hand, a loss of territory is liable to be a sore point in the future. Admittedly, in the light of later problems caused during the Hitler period by the loss of German territory, this may look like hindsight, but wars are seldom fought to retrieve lost revenue but to retrieve lost honor or lost territory.

B. **You push for the death penalty, in which Germany would pay substantial reparations and lose substantial territory. −2 points.** *The classic example of a vindictive solution, in which the gain is measured only by the increase in retribution to your opponent and your own payoffs are ignored—with an all-too-common consequence, as vindictive solutions frequently backfire.* This was in fact the solution imposed upon Germany by the Treaty of Versailles. While this may have seemed like a good idea to the Allies at the time, although it didn't to Wilson, the severe terms of the treaty were a major component in Hitler's rise to power, realizing the predictable adverse condequences the probabilities of which were ignored in the vindictive solution imposed at Versailles.

C. **You broker a compromise, in which the Germans would pay some reparations and lose some territory. 3 points.** While this may result in the Allies receiving an equivalent payoff to action A in terms of "punishment points," the residual bitterness that will be left by the loss of territory makes this action inferior.

WHAT ACTUALLY HAPPENED

The English and French imposed strict terms on the Germans, while the United States made separate arrangements. Fifteen years later, the Treaty of Versailles was shredded as part of Hitler's demands. This lesson was not lost on the World War II

Allies. Although the Russians used the lessons learned to divide Germany into separate regions, the West made efforts to enable West Germany to achieve stability and prosperity—a triumph for decision theory and learning from past experience.

What You Can Learn from History

Imposed punishment in just measure for a deserved crime stands a good chance of achieving the goal; a vindictive solution involving excessive punishment leaves a residue that the passage of time fails to erase. A dog who is punished for making a mess on the carpet learns not to do so, but one that is excessively punished becomes ill-tempered and hostile.

The other side of the coin is that there can be negative consequences from failing to impose a vindictive solution—and not just for large organizations such as Colossal Chips in the first quiz in this chapter. No teacher really likes to flunk a student, and no parent really likes to spank a child, but if the rod is too often spared, the child is very likely to be spoiled.

You've got to be really careful when you select a vindictive solution. The injunction in *The Mikado* to let the punishment fit the crime is an extremely wise one. Too harsh a solution frequently backfires, and too mild a punishment can also have adverse consequences. However, just as a golfer is advised to miss putts on the high side, it is possibly wiser to err on the side of leniency than on the side of severity. In fact, doing so is essentially a minimax approach to the problem of the severity of the vindictive solution; greater damage results from those who seek revenge than from those who feel entitled.

The Acid Test

We've come to the end of the first part of the journey. Hopefully, you've now acquired some of the important tools of decision theory—and been entertained in the process. The acid test, of course, is how you apply these tools in making the decisions that will impact your life. However, you might want to see how well you would do under simulated "battle conditions" by moving on to the second part of the book, in which there are four weeks of quizzes (at a rate of a quiz a day) to sharpen your skills. Like the decisions in real life, the quizzes come with no chapter headings to give you a clue as to what to expect.

PART 2

The Quizzes

As I said in the introduction, there's no better way to improve your decision-making abilities than to actually make decisions. Following is a four-week plan to test your decision-making mettle. Keep track of your score on each quiz, and add the scores up at the end of each week, or whenever you complete the seven quizzes for the week. If this were a course, I'd supply letter grades, but since this isn't, here's a more informal approach. Keep a running total of how you do on a week-by-week basis. (Use the scorecard that follows.) Hopefully, you should see improvement. In many activities, the learning curve shows sudden gains followed by periods of consolidation and retracement—if you play golf, your golf handicap won't come down smoothly, either. At the end of the four weeks, I'll supply an estimate for how you've done.

TITLE	SCORE	TITLE	SCORE
WEEK 1		**WEEK 2**	
Family Business	_____	Simply Shocking	_____
Instead of Flowers	_____	Home Improvement	_____
South of the Border	_____	The Baddest Part of Town	_____
West Coast Offense	_____	Facing the Facts	_____
The Cure	_____	Next Move	_____
Big Brother	_____	Uphill Battle	_____
Japanese Invasion	_____	Hornet's Nest	_____
Week 1 Total	_____	Week 2 Total	_____

TITLE	SCORE	TITLE	SCORE
WEEK 3		**WEEK 4**	
Copy This	_____	Dot-Com Redux	_____
Drama Queen	_____	Poison Pill	_____
Personnel Problem	_____	Anniversary Tea Leaves	_____
Wedding Bell Blues	_____	Conscience-Stricken	_____
Adrenaline Rush	_____	Jeans Blues	_____
Nine Lives	_____	Empire Builder	_____
The Hunchback	_____	OS Wars	_____
Week 3 Total	_____	Week 4 Total	_____
		Total for 4 Weeks	_____

WEEK 1, Quiz 1

Family Business

When you married the boss's daughter, there were a lot of wagging tongues—especially when you were made a vice president. Everyone now agrees that you've done a terrific job. Sales have increased, production is up, and the workplace environment is happy. However, there's a potential fly in the ointment—your father-in-law (aka the boss) has decided it would be a good idea to hire his nephew, who has graduated from somewhere with a degree in business. Obviously, you acquiesced, but a job interview convinced you that his nephew had perhaps the highest ratio of self-esteem to actual worth you had ever encountered. Nonetheless, you have to put this guy somewhere—if only to maintain peace in the family. Should you assign him to

A. analyzing sales trends?
B. analyzing hiring procedures?
C. analyzing employee medical plans?

SOLUTIONS: *Family Business*

A. You give him a job analyzing sales trends. —3 points.
The primary payoffs of a company are measured in *money*, and you can't afford to let this nitwit anywhere near the cash register. The influence of an individual tends to vary inversely with his or her distance to the head of the organization, and because he's the boss's nephew, people will listen to him. Don't give him—or them—the opportunity. *Decisions, such as this one, that are made using the minimax criterion involve accurately assessing the consequences of a major foul-up.*

B. You hire him for a position analyzing hiring procedures. —1 point. Part of what is producing those good primary payoffs is the morale of employees. Something is generating good office chemistry, and you simply cannot afford to have anything interfere with that. Because he's a relative of the boss, there's always the chance that someone will feel that something he says should be taken seriously—so make sure that if this is the case, it's on an issue much less critical than hiring.

C. You put him to work analyzing employee medical plans. 5 points. The clear winner. What's the worst that could happen? You switch from Alpha Dental to Beta Dental, or whatever. It's probably not true that when you've seen one employee health plan you've seen them all, but as long as employees get health benefits, they're probably not going to grumble a whole lot about which plan they're going to have to use.

Instead of Flowers

Your best friend, Helen, has passed away, after a long and happy life. Even though she was in her seventies, you always referred to her as Helen the Hippie because she hit her stride during the sixties as one of the original flower children from Haight-Ashbury. She never lost the sense of sweetness and innocence that characterized these times. The two of you might have had very different views on politics and philosophy, but your disagreements were always good-natured. Helen's family has requested that instead of flowers, you make a donation to an animal rights organization that Helen favored. You have major problems with this, as this organization strongly opposes medical experimentation using animals—a procedure resulting from such experimentation saved the life of another friend of yours. Should you

A. **honor their request and write a check to the animal rights organization?**

B. **find another organization of which both Helen and you would approve but that has nothing to do with animals and donate to them?**

C. **make a contribution to your local animal shelter?**

SOLUTIONS: *Instead of Flowers*

A. You honor their request and write a check to the animal rights organization. 1 point. This is a simple matter of counting. There are three parties involved here: you, Helen's family, and Helen's memory. You can be certain that doing this goes strongly against your core beliefs and equally certain that it is what Helen's family wants. But what would Helen want? She was your friend, and she would at least value your core beliefs as much as the charity preferred by the family.

B. You find another organization of which both Helen and you would approve but that has nothing to do with animals and donate to them. 2 points. This would satisfy both Helen and you but would probably not please Helen's family, as you are explicitly going against their wishes and making a point of doing so.

C. You make a contribution to your local animal shelter. 5 points. An easy winner. The welfare of animals was clearly important to Helen and is also important to her family. Unless the only animals you can abide are the virtual fish on your screensaver, it won't hurt you to contribute here—animal shelters unquestionably perform a useful function for the community. Unless Helen's family is among those people who firebomb the homes of medical researchers who use animals in their work, they will understand your objection to the particular charity they selected. *Sometimes it takes a little thought to find a creative action to resolve a decision, so when no alternative seems attractive, it's time to look outside of the box defined by the alternatives you are considering.*

WEEK 1, Quiz 3

South of the Border

You're not yet at the level of the Golden Arches or the Colonel—or even Starbucks—but your chain of franchised restaurants now extends from sea to shining sea and has hundreds of restaurants worldwide, although most are located in large cities. As you review the balance sheets, you notice that your results are regional in nature. You are doing amazingly well in the United States and Europe and have large profits from these areas. The few restaurants that you have in Asia also show large profits, but Central America and South America are disasters. The restaurants don't seem to be catching on there—at least from the standpoint of profit and loss—but you don't know why; it could be a poor economy or mismanagement or out-and-out corruption. You need to formulate a policy to deal with the black hole south—and far south—of the border. Should you

- **A. sell the restaurants, leave Central America and South America, and go where you're loved?**
- **B. spend some money for a team of auditors to see if they can pin down the weak spots?**
- **C. spend more money to replace local management with proven winners in your organization who are likely to get you an accurate read on the situation and turn a loser into a winner if it can be done?**

SOLUTIONS: *South of the Border*

A. You decide to sell the restaurants, leave Central America and South America, and go where you're loved. 2 points. Even though this is a give-up play, it may be the right one. Your restaurants are doing well in every other locale, so there is some reason for the failures in Central America and South America that may be idiosyncratic—and uncorrectable. As they say in poker, you have to know when to hold 'em—and when to fold 'em.

B. You spend some money for a team of auditors to see if they can pin down the weak spots. 0 points. OK, let's say this plan succeeds, and they locate the weak spots. Then what? You're either going to decide to pull out, in which case you would have spent more money than with option A, or you're going to try and improve the situation by sending in the shock troops, as in option C. But there's also the chance that the problem can't be found simply by auditing, and if that's the case, you wasted your money. This option is clearly inadmissible in comparison with either of the other alternatives.

C. You spend more money to replace local management with proven winners in your organization who are likely to get you an accurate read on the situation and turn a loser into a winner if it can be done. 5 points. People in America, Europe, and Asia like your food. Tasty food brings people into restaurants—and all over the world, people like different cuisines. Something's going on here, and it looks as if you're going to have to be in closer touch with what's happening in order to turn things around. There's no guarantee, but it certainly seems that your odds are good, and turning losers into winners is such a good result that it's worth the investment. *The reward/risk ratio of spending a little more money trying to become a winner is generally greater than the reward/risk ratio of spending a little less money trying to determine why you are a loser.*

West Coast Offense

You led a small college football team to an undefeated season and an unprecedented appearance in a bowl game, where they surprised everyone by upsetting a traditional football powerhouse that was having a poor year. As so often happens, the major schools came calling, and you accepted the head coaching position with a well-known football school that was going through hard times. When you arrived, you found that recruiting hadn't gone so well, and you were left with mostly freshmen and sophomores. You installed a high-powered version of the West Coast offense, and the team rebounded (somewhat) to a 7–5 season. Nonetheless, a vocal segment of the alumni are screaming for your head. You've got to plan what to do for the upcoming season and are faced with three choices.

A. **Accept a position as an offensive coordinator for one of the professional teams; it's about the same amount of money, but there will be considerably less pressure.**

B. **Rely on the fact that your team has now matured by one year, they are more familiar with the offense, and they should be able to improve on last year's record.**

C. **Switch to a more conventional offense that isn't as complicated and rely on the added maturity of your players to improve on last year's performance.**

SOLUTIONS: *West Coast Offense*

A. You accept a position as an offensive coordinator for one of the professional teams; it's about the same amount of money, but there will be considerably less pressure.
−1 point. You're on the verge of establishing yourself as a successful major college coach. This is a high-profile position with lots of perks, so why would you want to exchange it for something that is probably equally insecure with no profile and few perks? This is clearly inferior to staying with your current position.

B. You rely on the fact that your team has now matured by one year, they are more familiar with the offense, and they should be able to improve on last year's record.
5 points. You took a young team, installed a complicated offense that they didn't know, and showed a profit over the previous year's performance. There's a learning curve associated with any change and to bail now would be to throw everything that you've learned out the window. *You can only tell that you've reached the point of diminishing returns when your returns actually start diminishing.*

C. You switch to a more conventional offense that isn't as complicated and rely on the added maturity of your players to improve on last year's performance. 1 point.
While staying in your current position is a better career move, changing horses in midstream is the wrong thing to do. In addition to refusing to benefit from what you've learned, you're going to appear indecisive, and indecisive leaders generally do not evoke a whole lot of confidence from the organizations they lead. Plans should be changed when they have failed, not because they have only partially succeeded, and the final results are not yet in.

WEEK 1, Quiz 5

The Cure

It's been three decades since the plague that is AIDS first appeared, but finally there is some really good news: a research lab in your international pharmaceutical company has developed a cure. Instead of announcing it to the world, though, you've kept a really tight lid on the project, because a very peculiar fly has buzzed into the ointment (actually, it's in the genetically engineered intravenous injection that you have developed)—this particular cure works only on people with type O negative blood. Your scientists have spent nearly six months trying to get past this obstacle, and they've improved the success rate for other blood types, but there's still a huge disparity between how well it works on people with type O negative blood and how well it works on everyone else. Word of this has started to leak out, there have been bloggers speculating on developments in this area, and it looks like you're going to have to make some sort of move. Should you

A. **spend some more time trying to develop a cure that works independently of blood type?**
B. **patent the formula as is?**
C. **release your findings, make the formula public property, and simply manufacture the formula and market it?**

SOLUTIONS: *The Cure*

A. You decide to spend some more time trying to develop a cure that works independently of blood type. −2 points. This is a total loser from both a business and a humanitarian standpoint. In the interim, somebody else might come up with a cure and patent it. You can't afford to be second. Additionally, people who might be saved by your treatment could die if you don't bring it to market ASAP.

B. You patent the formula as is. 2 points. You have a product that is in demand. You are entitled to a return on your investment.

C. You release your findings, make the formula public property, and simply manufacture the formula and market it. 5 points. Talk about having your cake and eating it, too! You will be applauded for your humanitarianism, *and* you will undoubtedly make a tidy profit because your name will be associated with the drug and you'll get to market first! *Sometimes a move that results in an apparent reduction of payoffs, such as the humanitarian "giveaway" here, is actually the best Bayes' Criterion solution to the problem.*

Big Brother

Despite the fact that you licked them in the War of Independence and fought them to a draw in the War of 1812, the British are still a lot stronger than you are. So when the British foreign minister approaches you, President James Monroe, and says that he would like to make you an offer you can't refuse, you sit there and listen. The British foreign minister is suggesting that now would be a good time to let bygones be bygones and come up with a joint declaration on hemispheric policy. That's *your* hemisphere he's talking about, not his—his is still shaking off the effects of fifteen years of Napoleon-induced conflicts. While it might be nice to have a big brother, such a declaration would upset the Russians, who own Alaska and have established colonies almost as far south as San Francisco. The French and Spanish probably wouldn't be too keen on it, either. It's beginning to look like George Washington may have been right when, in his farewell address, he cautioned the country to avoid entangling alliances so that America could grow and develop on its own. On the other hand, having Britain as an ally would have advantages—it would at least give you some support if you run into troubles with other countries. With all this in mind, should you

A. **work together with Britain to formulate some sort of a policy regarding European involvement in this hemisphere?**

B. **support a policy of passive neutrality, in which you reaffirm Washington's principle of avoiding entangling alliances?**

C. **formulate a policy of aggressive neutrality, in which you tell all the European powers to mind their own business?**

SOLUTIONS: *Big Brother*

A. You work together with Britain to formulate some sort of a policy regarding European involvement in this hemisphere. 1 point. Your payoffs here are determined by what's best for America, and what's probably best for America is to be allowed to develop unhindered. An alliance might seriously complicate the achievement of that objective by giving England a strong voice in the hemisphere. *Forming a coalition with a stronger partner is valuable when there is a visible immediate benefit or protection from a threat that is either immediate or has significant potential.* The Mafia can collect protection money precisely because it can offer protection from a threat—even though the Mafia itself is the threat.

B. You support a policy of passive neutrality, in which you reaffirm Washington's principle of avoiding entangling alliances. 2 points. This is a step in the right direction. The balance of power that exists in Europe will work to your advantage, as the different powers will realize that they can't count on any help from you. The one problem here is that a European power might decide to try to further its interests away from Europe on the theory that such a move is less likely to be viewed by the other European posers as hostile in the same way a similar move made in Europe would be.

C. You formulate a policy of aggressive neutrality, in which you tell the European powers to mind their own business. 5 points. Now you have not only made the balance of power in Europe work to your advantage by declaring neutrality, you have lessened their payoffs for aggressive moves in your hemisphere by announcing that you will oppose such moves, no matter who makes them. This will significantly decrease the probability of such detrimental moves.

WHAT ACTUALLY HAPPENED

President Monroe chose to formulate a policy of aggressive neutrality, which basically let the European powers know that America would not interfere in European affairs and that European powers should not interfere in America's affairs. This policy, which shortly became known as the Monroe Doctrine, is still in force and was called upon as recently as the 1963 Cuban missile crisis.

What You Can Learn from History

An alliance, or any organization from the PTA up through NATO, should be formed with a purpose. If there's no purpose, the organization tends to look for things to do to justify its existence. There are some extremely good (and extremely humorous) books on this subject, from C. Northcote Parkinson's *The Parkinson Principle* to John Gall's *Systemantics*.

Japanese Invasion

It's the 1970s, and General Motors has been consistently profitable for almost seventy years, thanks to its basic strategy of one model for every economic level. Driving a Chevy or a Cadillac immediately identifies who you are—at least in economic terms. However, this strategy has suddenly taken a beating. Soaring gasoline prices have caused consumers to see your larger cars as gas guzzlers, and the Japanese are attacking—not with dive bombers but with low-priced, fuel-efficient cars. They have the advantage of more modern manufacturing techniques because they can basically start from scratch, whereas you have a lot of money invested in your factories. This is the gravest threat the company has faced in three-quarters of a century—but fortunately, you're cash-rich and can marshal a lot of money to back whatever changes you decide need to be made. Should you

A. adopt techniques such as plant automation to make your existing cars more competitive with regard to features the customers seem to be demanding, such as fuel economy?

B. go head-to-head with the Japanese by bringing out a new family of low-priced, fuel-efficient cars?

C. look to strengthen areas in which you have a strong position, such as trucks and minivans, as well as searching for possible new product lines?

SOLUTIONS: *Japanese Invasion*

A. **You adopt techniques such as plant automation to make your existing cars more competitive with regard to features the customers seem to be demanding, such as fuel economy. 2 points.** This doesn't seem to be an unreasonable idea, as you'll probably have to retool eventually anyway. However, this is a defensive move in a situation in which you need to score some victories.

B. **You go head-to-head with the Japanese by bringing out a new family of low-priced, fuel-efficient cars. −2 points.** You are essentially acknowledging that the enemy has taken command of this field, and you are trying to beat him on his own turf. If you bring out a low-priced Cadillac, you may well alienate the Cadillac buyers who see the Cadillac as a symbol of their success.

C. **You look to strengthen areas in which you have a strong position, such as trucks and minivans, as well as searching for possible new product lines. 5 points.** Sometimes you just have to take your lumps. *However, a multidimensional entity can often look to score victories in areas other than ones in which it has recently absorbed a defeat.* We do this as well—when things aren't going so well with our love life, we can look to improve things on the job, at school, or in our leisure-time activities.

WHAT ACTUALLY HAPPENED

GM made the unfortunate mistake of choosing to attempt overnight automation of its factories and essentially threw thirty billion dollars down the drain, which it could certainly have used as the curtain came down on 2008. It would have been much better served to have concentrated on trucks and minivans—and might even have brought out the SUV (sports utility vehicle) sooner.

WEEK 2, Quiz 1

Simply Shocking

One of the more uncomfortable facts that society has had to face is that crimes of violence periodically go on an upswing. Women in particular are frequent targets of crimes of violence, and after your wife was nearly mugged, you decided that it was time to do something about it. You remembered the catchphrase of 2007, "Don't tase me, bro," purchased a Taser, and did some tinkering. The result of your tinkering convinced you that you could come up with some significant improvements on the civilian model, but if you implemented all of them, the result would be a weapon that could probably only be purchased by the rich and famous, who already have bodyguards protecting them. You have to decide which feature to focus on. Should you use your improvements to

A. reduce the price, offering a stun gun comparable to the standard Taser but costing $250 as opposed to $350?
B. double the range at which the stun gun is effective?
C. significantly increase the stopping power of the stun gun?

SOLUTIONS: *Simply Shocking*

A. You reduce the price, offering a stun gun comparable to the standard Taser but costing $250 as opposed to $350. −1 point. Price reductions almost always will bring in extra customers—but this may be the exception that proves the rule. A person who buys a stun gun does so because he or she feels threatened, and the extra $100 is a drop in the bucket when it comes to purchasing peace of mind.

B. You double the range at which the weapon is effective. 1 point. This is a feature that might be of interest to a prospective purchaser, as it would increase the area in which the purchaser would feel safe. But how important is it? If you felt your life was in danger, you'd want a gun, which is much more effective over a much greater range. A Taser is a defensive weapon, primarily for close-in situations.

C. You significantly increase the stopping power of the weapon. 5 points. Right on target. The purchaser of such a weapon wants to buy enough time to get the hell out of danger, and this is the critical feature. The minimax criterion is used when you want to lessen the risk of a worst-case scenario, and that's precisely what increasing the stopping power of the weapon does. *When you don't even want to think about what's the worst thing that could happen, that's when you should think about the worst thing that could happen.*

WEEK 2, Quiz 2

Home Improvement

A backyard pool. Redoing the patio. A new kitchen. All of these improve the *house*, but absolutely nothing upgrades the *home* as much as improvements to the husband. You have to admit that your husband is pretty damned good, as husbands go. He brings home the bacon, he's good with the kids, and only once in seven years of marriage has he forgotten either your anniversary or your birthday. Still, maybe it's the seven-year-itch thing, but you feel there are improvements that could be made on the husband front. He often dresses like a slob, and then there's the deal with the fact that you like the toilet seat down. Nonetheless, it's a good marriage, and you'd hate to be seen as a nag. Should you

A. wait until he finds something to complain about and then suggest that you each have aspects you could improve?

B. let sleeping dogs lie and accept the status quo of a good marriage?

C. wait until a special occasion, such as your anniversary, and then tell him that instead of flowers what you'd really like is for him to leave the toilet seat down, etc.?

SOLUTIONS: *Home Improvement*

A. You wait until he finds something to complain about and then suggest that you each have aspects you could improve. 5 points. If you go about this correctly, this has the best chance of improving everyone's payoffs. He'll get something, you'll get something, and the marriage will gain a lot. Smoothing out rough edges is one of the keys to a successful relationship, and modifying equilibrium solutions so that all parties obtain higher payoffs is the general framework under which this falls. *Achieving a new equilibrium with higher payoffs to both parties is possible when the parties are cooperating but almost impossible when the parties are competing.*

B. You let sleeping dogs lie and accept the status quo of a good marriage. 2 points. There is always a risk in trying to modify an acceptable equilibrium solution. There may be an equilibrium solution with higher payoffs, but you may find yourself incurring much lower payoffs in an attempt to move toward it.

C. You wait until a special occasion, such as your anniversary, and then tell him that instead of flowers what you'd really like is for him to leave the toilet seat down, etc. —2 points. Congratulations! You have just managed to turn a romantic, payoff-producing occasion into an unromantic, payoff-losing one. Moves like this are the stuff of which sitcom episodes are made, in which one party is immensely embarrassed, frostiness occurs, and finally everyone makes up at the end. Life may not be so eager to imitate art if you adopt this approach.

WEEK 2, Quiz 3

The Baddest Part of Town

The South Side of Chicago is indeed, as Jim Croce put it, the baddest part of town—in part because you control a moderate-size portion of it, where you operate a thriving business in illicit pharmaceuticals. You share this part of the Windy City in an uneasy truce with a rival organization, the Jets—but things are about to change. Another big organization, the Sharks, is considering an expansion to the South Side, and almost certainly a turf war between the Jets and the Sharks will result. Everyone suspects that you will ally with the Sharks in the coming conflict, many of whose top executives are friends from your youth, but meanwhile there has been an unusual development. You control the traffic in a pharmaceutical that is in short supply. A high-ranking member of the Jets has proposed a purchasing agreement rather than a battle for territory, and doing this is almost certain to antagonize the Sharks. You've only been able to come up with three possible options.

A. Form what seems to be an inevitable alliance with the Sharks and pass on the deal with the Jets.

B. Try to keep your nose clean by passing on the deal with the Jets but let it be known that you want to stay out of the coming turf war.

C. Accept the deal with the Jets—after all, business is business.

SOLUTIONS: *The Baddest Part of Town*

A. You form what seems to be an inevitable alliance with the Sharks and pass on the deal with the Jets. −2 points. Although this is seemingly a highly complex situation, once you focus on your payoffs, the answer becomes crystal clear. What you need are time and money—time to see what's going to happen, and rich or poor, it's nice to have money. Choose this action and say goodbye to the money while simultaneously exacerbating the chances of a conflict.

B. You try to keep your nose clean by passing on the deal with the Jets but let it be known that you want to stay out of the coming turf war. 2 points. This is certainly better than the previous action, in that it can buy you time. If the Sharks decide to pass, you can reopen negotiations. At any rate, you won't have precipitated hostilities by this action.

C. You accept the deal with the Jets—after all, business is business. 5 points. It's an ironic situation. You can be virtually certain that this deal will eventually be broken. So can the Jets, but they are inking the deal for exactly the same reason that you are. They want to buy time to prepare for a turf war against the Sharks and would like to increase their financial resources to prepare for it. This action generates an equilibrium solution for both you and the Jets until the moment that the Sharks decide to move in. At that point, the actions defined by your drug deal will no longer define an equilibrium solution to a game, which will then have evolved from cooperation to competition. *An unstable equilibrium is often preferable to no equilibrium at all.*

WEEK 2, Quiz 4

Facing the Facts

You've been a competitive basketball player all your life—in fact, you went to college on a basketball scholarship. Few make the transition to the NBA, and you were forced to acknowledge that a career in the pros was simply not in the cards. Nonetheless, you've held your own with the youngsters at the gym—and you're in your forties. However, you find yourself getting sidelined with injuries now that you never suffered when you were younger, and a hip injury is just healing. You have no intention of giving up athletics, which have played such an important role in your life, but you have to face the facts: Father Time is catching up with you. Should you

A. play with the same intensity as always, risking injuries due to the fact that age is taking its toll?

B. not give the proverbial 110 percent and instead settle for 100 percent? Or 90 percent? Or maybe 80 percent?

C. switch to another sport that is less physically demanding, such as golf?

SOLUTIONS: *Facing the Facts*

A. **You decide to play with the same intensity as always, risking injuries due to the fact that age is taking its toll. 2 points.** You could get lucky. You don't have to get injured, and you might be able to go for quite a while giving it your all. On the other hand, you have to face up to the fact that you are increasing the chance of doing major damage that might sideline you—permanently.

B. **You don't give the proverbial 110 percent and instead settle for 100 percent or less. 5 points**. Your goal here is to continue to play hoops, for as long as possible. It's your game. You can still play, but you just won't go as hard to the hoop, and you're going to get dunked on occasionally. *Your long-term payoffs here are to play long-term, and the Bayes' Criterion is applied when you recognize that you're in it for the long haul.*

C. **You switch to another sport that is less physically demanding, such as golf. 0 points.** How do you know you'll like golf? Or be good at it? Worse, if you find out that either you don't care for the game or you're a terrible golfer, you'll have spent a bunch of money and wasted a lot of time, and you'll find it harder to get back into hoops, even at a reduced level of effort. You're exchanging certain payoffs for dubious ones, rarely a wise move, especially when they're likely to be lower payoffs, even in a best-case scenario in which you like golf and are pretty good at it.

Next Move

You are the owner of a small Swiss chemical firm that manufactures textile dyes. It's just after the conclusion of the Great War—World War I, although you don't yet know that another world war will follow—and business is not so good. You're trying to compete against the giant German chemical firms, and even though you have some accounts and the prospect of more, you know that it's going to be an uphill struggle. Suddenly, what could be an incredible opportunity has presented itself. All the German firms have passed on the opportunity to develop vitamins, recently discovered substances in food that have nutritional value—a deficiency in vitamin C, for instance, is the cause of scurvy, and rickets is often the result of deficiency in vitamin D. Nonetheless, there is the nagging worry that the German giants are no fools, and they must have had a good reason for passing on this one. Should you

A. take the information you have gained from the German firms and try to improve your business by hiring top-flight salesmen?

B. take the plunge, buy up the vitamin patents, and concentrate on manufacturing and marketing them?

C. get your feet wet by manufacturing and test-marketing vitamins while simultaneously maintaining your chemical business?

SOLUTIONS: *Next Move*

A. You take the information you have gained from the German firms and try to improve your business by hiring top-flight salesmen. 1 point. You have to take some steps to make matters better, and the German firms have obviously looked at the opportunity to develop and be at the forefront of the vitamin industry carefully and decided it's not worth the effort—to them. Good salesmen are almost invariably worth more than what they're paid, so this should help you improve the bottom line, at least for now.

B. You take the plunge, buy up the vitamin patents, and concentrate on manufacturing and marketing them. 5 points. This would take a lot of courage—but faint heart ne'er won fair lady. *There are two times that you should take a large risk— when you have very little to lose and when you can afford to lose.* This may be the only opportunity you will ever see to really hit it big, and you will never stop kicking yourself if you see vitamins developing into a significant industry.

C. You get your feet wet by manufacturing and test-marketing vitamins while simultaneously maintaining your chemical business. −1 point. You can't afford to split your forces. If you simply nibble at the vitamin market, the big German firms could see success on the horizon and swoop in. This could also detract from what business you currently have. You have to fish or cut bait.

WHAT ACTUALLY HAPPENED

Maybe you've heard of Hoffmann-La Roche, the giant Swiss pharmaceutical firm that now controls much of the world's supply of vitamins—as well as other pharmaceuticals. This is their story—because they bought up the vitamin patents.

This story hits uncomfortably close to home, because a member of my family faced a similar decision at approximately the same time. My Uncle Edwin was approached by two brothers who wanted $500 (a not-insignificant sum at that time) for a half-interest in their cosmetic firm. Uncle Edwin thought it over, passed, and used the $500 to buy paintings of cats. The brothers were Charles and Martin Revson, and the firm was Revlon.

WEEK 2, Quiz 6

Uphill Battle

It's the summer of 1948, Harry Truman, and the task ahead of you looks almost impossible. It started two years ago, when the Republicans seized control of Congress during the off-year election, setting themselves up as the favorite for the upcoming presidential election. They nominated Thomas Dewey, popular former governor of New York (with its huge number of electoral votes) and a seasoned campaigner after his defeat by Franklin Roosevelt in the 1944 election. As if these weren't problems enough, the Democratic Party has been split into not two, but three factions. The sizeable ultra-liberal contingent has formed the Progressive Party and nominated Henry Wallace for president. The Southern Democrats, a smaller segment infuriated by the civil rights plank in the Democratic platform, have also split off, running Strom Thurmond at the head of a Southern Democratic party that the press has taken to calling the Dixiecrats. Despite all this, you have told the press and everyone who will listen that you are going to pull off a mammoth upset. Are you simply whistling in the dark, or does your master plan entail

A. **a reconciliation with the Progressive Party, which will alienate the Dixiecrats even further but could swing some crucial northern states?**

B. **a behind-the-scenes deal with the Dixiecrats in the hope of gaining the solid South's bloc of electoral votes and moving on from there?**

C. **no wheeling or dealing but instead relying on just good hard work and a belief that the Republicans are counting unhatched chickens?**

SOLUTIONS: *Uphill Battle*

A. You reconcile with the Progressive Party, which will alienate the Dixiecrats even further but could swing some crucial northern states. 1 point. If you are going to form a coalition, this is your best bet, as you could regard the Dixiecrats as a lost cause anyway. However, it isn't clear that a coalition will give you the necessary payoffs because it looks like you need every vote you can get.

B. You broker a behind-the-scenes deal with the Dixiecrats in the hope of gaining the solid South's bloc of electoral votes and moving on from there. −1 point. You are still playing the coalition game but not as effectively as before. *There are times when it is correct to form a coalition with a weak partner, but this tactic works best when the combined strength of the coalition exceeds the strength of the opposition.*

C. You eschew all the wheeling or dealing and instead rely on just good hard work and a belief that the Republicans are counting unhatched chickens. 5 points. As has already been observed, forming a coalition in this situation is liable to be counterproductive, so your best bet is to tough it out on your own and hope that the Dixiecrats and the Progressives realize that it's better to see a Democrat that they know in the White House than a Dewey they don't.

WHAT ACTUALLY HAPPENED

The newspapers had already hit the streets with their "Dewey Defeats Truman" headlines on election night, but when the nation woke up the next morning, Truman had pulled off the biggest upset in American political history. Many elections have turned on the results of coalitions, but this was one that may have depended on the coalitions that weren't formed. Truman was smart enough not to form an alliance with either the Progressives or the Dixiecrats and thus avoided losing votes from those who were sitting on the fence.

What You Can Learn from History

You don't have to make a deal with a person who has no other options. If you want your teenage daughter to wash the dishes as part of her daily responsibilities to the household, and she thinks you ought to give her an iPod for doing so, where's she going to go? You may decide to give her the iPod anyway, but make it clear that it wasn't because she negotiated it.

Hornet's Nest

You're a former phone company executive, Randall Tobias, who appears to have stepped into a hornet's nest. The giant pharmaceutical firm Eli Lilly has suffered huge losses in the last year, and you have been hired as the new CEO. Arriving on your first day of work, you find that rumors of massive layoffs are circulating, with an obviously debilitating effect on productivity. The financial community is looking at your balance sheet and is demanding action to restore profitability. If all this weren't bad enough, the trial of a promising new hepatitis drug has taken a catastrophic turn for the worse, as several patients have become seriously ill. You can't deal with all these issues simultaneously. At last count there were only twenty-four hours in a day. What should you do first?

A. Tackle the financial problems at the firm by looking for productive and nonproductive divisions and weeding out the weak sisters.

B. Check on the status of the hepatitis drug and make sure that the health of the patients is the primary focus of the company.

C. Concentrate on restoring employee confidence in order to maintain organizational stability and productivity.

SOLUTIONS: *Hornet's Nest*

A. You tackle the financial problems at the firm by looking for productive and nonproductive divisions and weeding out the weak sisters. 1 point. This is definitely something that needs to be done for the long-term viability of the company—but it's a lengthy project and not one that needs to be done immediately. Besides, concentrating on this will probably exacerbate the worries of the employees (especially those who feel they are in weak-sister divisions) and certainly won't do anything to build public confidence in your company as a pharmaceutical manufacturer.

B. You immediately check on the status of the hepatitis drug and make sure that the health of the patients is the primary focus of the company. 5 points. This is the clear winner in the priority sweepstakes. Your survival as a pharmaceutical firm depends largely on two things—the quality of your pharmaceuticals and the trust the public has in them. The former may not matter if the latter disappears. Remember thalidomide? Love Canal? *Whether you are a company or an individual, any decision that reduces the trust others have in you is likely to reduce other payoffs as well.*

C. You concentrate on restoring employee confidence in order to maintain organizational stability and productivity. −1 point. Just how are you going to do this in a vacuum? Words alone cannot do this. Actions must be taken to restore not only the confidence of the public but the confidence of the employees. Showing that you are focused on the primary mission of the company will help restore the confidence of the employees in the mission—and the company.

WHAT ACTUALLY HAPPENED

Tobias made it clear that initially his primary concern was the well-being of the patients in the hepatitis trial. Although several patients died as a result of complications stemming from the drug, trust in Eli Lilly was gradually restored. Tobias also took measures to make the company more competitive by eliminating weak-sister divisions, and the company prospered through the remainder of the decade.

WEEK 3, Quiz 1

Copy This

It took a decade for Chester Carlson to get his idea to copy images using static electricity off the ground, but once Xerox made it off the runway, even the sky was not the limit. It's the middle of the 1970s, but you know you've made it when your corporate name becomes a verb, and now people say "Xerox this" rather than "Copy this." Your name is synonymous with copying, but there are other things to do in the office besides copying. Information comes into the office via telephone, is processed by computer, and is duplicated and shipped out via copying. You've got the copying leg locked up for now, but there's a small cloud on the horizon—Japanese companies are beginning to copy copiers, and companies such as Ricoh and Toshiba are nibbling at your heels. Nonetheless, if you could integrate an office to go all-Xerox, your bottom line would boom. AT&T seems to have the telephone input locked up, and even though these strange things called personal computers are starting to penetrate the market, IBM is still pre-eminent in office computers. What next? Should you

A. concentrate on making sure that Xerox remains synonymous with copying?

B. try to produce telephones to rival AT&T, as that's the cheaper item to produce?

C. try to produce computers, as they are the easier item to integrate with copiers?

SOLUTIONS: *Copy This*

A. You decide to concentrate on making sure that Xerox remains synonymous with copying. 5 points. There was a time when you had nowhere to go but up, and now is the time that you have nowhere to go but down. *When you have built an empire, there is a lot to lose—world domination hasn't been achieved since Alexander the Great.* This means that, as a dominant company, you must view your own expansion attempts very carefully, making sure that they do not distract you from protecting your rear flank.

B. You try to break into the telecommunications industry and produce telephones to rival AT&T, as that's the cheaper item to produce. −1 point. You'll lose less money if you fail in the telecommunications market than if you fail in the computer market, as computers are more expensive to produce—but you're almost certain to fail. Even if you produce a great telephone, when people think Xerox, they think copier, not telephone. Additionally, telephones do not make a natural fit with copiers. Even if it's easier for an auto company to manufacture a food mixer than a motorcycle, they're much more likely to succeed with the motorcycle.

C. You try to produce computers, as that's the easier item to integrate with copiers. 2 points. This isn't an unreasonable idea—if you succeed, you gain control of the vast majority of the modern office. But can you succeed? You're going up against IBM, a highly successful company, and you're faced with the same problem that a successful product might not be saleable, as people naturally think copiers when they think Xerox. Nonetheless, on a Bayes' Criterion basis this is a reasonable venture—the payoff from success more than justifies taking the chance as long as you make sure to protect your turf.

WHAT ACTUALLY HAPPENED

Xerox made several forays into the computer market—and got their corporate head handed to them. Not only did they not manage any notable penetration of the computer market, they found that the Japanese copier companies that were at first mere blips on the horizon soon evolved into major threats. The decision to go after computers has come under criticism from several business gurus, but these criticisms have the aura of hindsight being notably more accurate than foresight. Possibly some minor tweaking, either with the computer that Xerox developed, the advertising campaign they adopted, or the sales incentives they offered might have made the difference.

Drama Queen

You saw your first movie when you were three years old, and you instantly knew what you wanted to do: be a movie star (you and approximately twenty million others). The odds are no longer twenty million to one against; you've recently graduated with a degree in drama (you and maybe one million others) and starred in your college productions, and every so often someone asks you if you're Angelina Jolie's sister (you and very few others). With all this going for you, you've decided to turn down your father's offer of a position in his plumbing-supply business and take your show on the road. You're mulling over three possibilities. Should you

A. take an offer to be an understudy to the lead in a revival of *My Fair Lady* in Chicago?

B. take a leading role in a performance of *Phantom of the Opera* in Charleston, South Carolina?

C. head for Hollywood, where you know absolutely no one, and make a living as a waitress while waiting for that one big break?

SOLUTIONS: *Drama Queen*

A. You take an offer to be an understudy to the lead in a revival of *My Fair Lady* in Chicago. 1 point. Here's the best-case scenario with this option—let's suppose that, in the great tradition of the theater, you say to the lead, "Break a leg"—and she does so. You take over the leading role, to accolades from all the critics. Then what? You either continue in Chicago, marry a commodities broker, and live happily (or unhappily) ever after—or you pack up your belongings, take that review, and join thousands of others in Hollywood.

B. You take a leading role in a performance of *Phantom of the Opera* in Charleston, South Carolina. 3 points. This is clearly superior to being an understudy, as you don't have to rely on someone breaking a leg. *As a result, being an understudy is inadmissible when compared with this option, and inadmissible actions must be eliminated from consideration.* However, after *Phantom* completes its run (if it ever does), you're in the identical position as before.

C. You head for Hollywood, where you know absolutely no one, and make a living as a waitress while waiting for that one big break. 5 points. Your chances of being discovered in Hollywood are much greater than they are anywhere else—because that's where people get discovered. You can either try to be a big fish in the ocean or settle for being a big fish in a small puddle (no disrespect intended to either Chicago or Charleston, but they're not the capital of the film industry; Hollywood is). You could have a successful career elsewhere, but you'd always wonder about whether or not you could have fulfilled a childhood dream. Even if you fall flat, you've got to take a shot. It is better to have loved and lost than never to have loved at all, because love is where the big-time payoffs are.

Personnel Problem

Your father, Henry Ford, founded the Ford Motor Company, and after he handed the reins over to you, Ford continued to be one of the Big Three, the leading car producers in the United States. You wouldn't mind consulting him for guidance, but he passed away nearly thirty years ago, and so it's up to you to make the call on this one. A year before your father died, a bright young engineer named Lee Iacocca joined the company and quickly turned into one of its driving (pardon the pun) forces. He was responsible for your highly successful Mustang, and even though he stumbled slightly with the Pinto, he's done a terrific job as Ford's president. But you're the CEO, and you just can't stand the man. He's modern, you're traditional, he's Italian, you're Anglo-Saxon—and a whole bunch of other things that he is, you're not—and vice versa. Should you

- **A. bite your lip and let sleeping dogs lie?**
- **B. promote him sideways by offering him inducements to take over the underperforming European branch of Ford Motors?**
- **C. fire him?**

SOLUTIONS: *Personnel Problem*

A. You bite your lip and let sleeping dogs lie. 2 points. Ever heard the saying "If it ain't broke, don't fix it"? It ain't broke—as a matter of fact it's doing quite well. This situation recurs frequently, as often there's a conflict between management and star performer, or ownership and management. Sometimes you have to recognize that ego should be subordinated to enterprise.

B. You promote him sideways by offering him inducements to take over the underperforming European branch of Ford Motors. 5 points. This creative approach solves two problems and takes a constructive step toward solving another— it keeps Iacocca with the company and allows him to use his undoubted talents to shore up a weak sister. That's one of the problems, and the constructive step. It also gets him out of your hair, which is another problem this move solves. *When there are conflicting systems of payoffs, there may (on rare occasions) be a win-win way to resolve them, and the gain is so large from doing so that it's worth spending time, money, and effort to look for it.*

C. You fire him. −3 points. Of course you would never even consider this. Not only would you lose your most valuable employee, the effect on company performance and morale could be devastating. People will be more concerned with not upsetting you than on doing a good job. It will be harder to hire good people, and the ones you have may start looking elsewhere. Is this what you want?

WHAT ACTUALLY HAPPENED

Unbelievable as it may seem, Henry Ford II fired Lee Iacocca, uttering the classic line, "I just don't like you very much," while doing so. Chrysler Corporation, which had been on the verge of bankruptcy, snapped up Iacocca and made him the chairman. Iacocca almost immediately turned Chrysler around, bringing many of his former colleagues at Ford in to help with the rebuilding—you might have thought Henry II could have foreseen this. It should come as no surprise that, at the same time that Chrysler rebounded, Ford tanked.

What You Can Learn from History

When you're in charge, whether of a family or an organization, you should realize that the sum of the payoffs of the group exceed the payoffs to you as an individual—unless, like Louis XIV or a dictator, you *are* the state.

WEEK 3, Quiz 4

Wedding Bell Blues

And you thought the big problem was getting her to say "yes"! You chose the time and the place, you had the ring ready, and it all went exactly according to the script. While still basking in the warm fuzzy afterglow of this momentous occasion, your intended proceeded to describe her dream wedding, a relatively modest affair with only close family and intimate friends—maybe fifty or so people. This didn't set well with either your parents or hers—although they're not about to rent a football stadium for the proceedings, they're envisioning something much more elaborate in the way of ceremony and celebration. Nobody asked you, but you'd just as soon ink the deal at City Hall and spend the money on a nice honeymoon. Oops, someone did just ask you—the blushing bride-to-be. Do you tell her that you prefer

A. **a quick trip to City Hall and a nice honeymoon?**
B. **an elaborate ceremony and celebration, as the parents seem to want?**
C. **a small wedding, as she prefers?**

SOLUTIONS: *Wedding Bell Blues*

A. You tell her you'd like to make a quick trip to City Hall and go on a nice honeymoon. −3 points. *Honesty is the best policy—most of the time. The big trick is to recognize the exceptions.* It's not your payoffs that matter in this instance; at most weddings the groom is an afterthought. This is a great way to get things off on the wrong foot. If by some chance you get your way here, you are going to hear about this from everyone for the rest of your life.

B. You try to convince her that you're enthusiastic about an elaborate ceremony and celebration, as the parents seem to want. 2 points. They're paying for it, and if they manage to talk your sweetheart into going this route, so be it.

C. You tell her you want a small wedding, as she prefers. 5 points. Your payoffs are her payoffs on this once-in-a-lifetime event. The bride is the star at the wedding, and the best way to ensure that she will do her best to make you happy throughout the course of the marriage is to do your best to make her happy on her wedding day—by letting her have her way on as many details pertaining to the wedding as possible.

Adrenaline Rush

You were among the first to sense the appeal of extreme sports nearly twenty years ago, back when it was just a bunch of kids on skateboards with expressions like "rad." It's absolutely amazing the way the industry has grown, and now extreme sports have gotten their own television series, worked their way into the Olympics, boosted the sales of gear such as mountain bikes, and even spawned lines of apparel. The industry, amazingly enough, is still expanding, as people find new and exciting ways of putting life and limb on the line. Your problem is that your division heads came along at the same time you did. They've ridden the initial wave, but can you trust geezers in their late thirties to be on the cutting edge (possibly a literal expression, as extreme fencing may be next)? What should you do to make sure your company keeps showing healthy profits as the industry moves forward? Should you

A. stick with your current crop of division heads and products?

B. stick with your current crop of division heads and do market research to determine the future direction of the company?

C. hire a newer and younger group to determine which way the company should go?

SOLUTIONS: *Adrenaline Rush*

A. You stick with your current crop of division heads and products. 2 points. Good. The industry is expanding, and a rising tide tends to float all boats. This move is unlikely to result in a catastrophe, and from a minimax standpoint, it would be the winner. *Minimax strategies are often moves that don't rock the boat, and if you are the industry leader in a growing industry, if the industry is not undergoing radical change, there is no necessity to rock the boat.* Additionally, since you're not making a catastrophic error, you can wait to see what happens and then climb on the bandwagon, even though you'll be a latecomer.

B. You stick with your current crop of division heads and do market research to determine the future direction of the company. 3 points. Better. You are sticking with people who have proven that they can succeed, and you are reducing the chances of making a mistake in determining future trends in extreme sports.

C. You hire a newer and younger group to determine which way the company should go. 5 points. Best. Extreme sports are growing *now*, they're a what's-happening-now industry, and so you need to find *now* people who will have the best information available. It's a maximax situation. This move might be dubious if the industry were stagnant or declining, as aggressive moves can be catastrophic in such situations, but that's not the case here. This is the time to shove more chips into the pot, but you've got to make sure that you're playing the right game. The best information you have is that extreme sports are primarily a pursuit of the young, not the young in heart. This is preferable to simply doing market research, because even though you'd undoubtedly gain useful information through market research, you'd prefer to have decisions being made by people who stand to profit by correct decisions.

Nine Lives

Ever since the century began, the man has caused you nothing but trouble. Nonetheless, it's hard not to admire Napoleon; he seems to have more lives than a cat! The Congress of Vienna, to which you are a delegate, is about to decide whether to put an end to the man, the myth, or perhaps both. It has taken five coalitions among the various European nations to defeat him. Even when he seemed to be stopped for good, he managed to escape from exile on the island of Elba off the coast of Italy in the Mediterranean Sea, where it took the Hundred Days' War to finally put an end to his adventures. Even so, the people of France still seem to be solidly behind him, and if it weren't for the fact that he has lost the support of the politicians, you might still be having nightmares about what he might do next. The good news is that he has surrendered to the captain of the British battleship *Bellerophon*, but the bad news is that you still have to decide what punishment you should mete out to him. Is it a matter of simply letting the punishment fit the crime, or after fifteen years of war, are you going to hold out for nothing more than minimizing potential future damage? All things considered, do you feel that it is best to

A. **execute him?**
B. **imprison him in one of the countries that has suffered most at his hands?**
C. **exile him once again, this time to a place that even a competent travel agent won't be able to find?**

SOLUTIONS: *Nine Lives*

A. You execute him. −2 points. If you were seeking a vindictive solution to the problem, this would obviously be the best action—as Archie Bunker so succinctly put it, revenge is the best way of getting even. However, vindictive solutions can also impose large negative payoffs on the decision maker. Such is certainly the case here. Napoleon is obviously still popular, and executing him could well make him a martyr. *Vindictive solutions, although sometimes extremely satisfying, are often two-edged swords. In business, for instance, it is often much more profitable in the long run to let a rival who has resisted a takeover continue to direct the business, rather than to remove him.*

B. You imprison him in one of the countries that has suffered most at his hands. 0 points. Also a vindictive solution, and one with a different set of drawbacks. If it took five different coalitions to defeat him, there are going to be a lot of different countries that might want the dubious honor of imprisoning him. Or will they? Knowing that Napoleon is in prison in Britain (or Austria or Prussia or Russia) might well make that nation a focus for potential hostile actions.

C. You exile him once again, this time to a place that even a competent travel agent won't be able to find. 5 points. While not ideal, you hope that by keeping him out of sight, you will be keeping him out of mind. Your interest in preserving long-term chances for peace in Europe makes the decision a matter of using the Bayes' Criterion. Although you can't be absolutely certain, this seems to be the best way to ensure that Napoleon, or the memory of Napoleon, does not have an impact on future developments.

WHAT ACTUALLY HAPPENED

Shortly after the Congress of Vienna, Napoleon was exiled to the island of St. Helena in the Atlantic Ocean, this time for keeps, and he died there of stomach cancer in 1821. As a result of the various deals worked out during the Congress of Vienna, an uneasy peace prevailed in Europe for approximately thirty years.

What You Can Learn from History

Vindictive solutions always have the potential for blowback. If you have to terminate something, a relationship or an employee, you can reduce the chances of blowback by trying to do it in as humane a manner as possible.

WEEK 3, Quiz 7

The Hunchback

As an executive with General Electric, you find yourself faced with a problem concerning one of your most important people. Charles Steinmetz has had an extraordinary career. He was a brilliant student in Germany, but his liberal ideas got him in trouble with Otto von Bismarck, the Iron Chancellor, and lucky for you, he had to emigrate. He is currently the chief of your calculating section, the people who used to spend their workdays doing what your pocket calculator now does. Although he stands barely over four feet tall, there is no question that although he may physically be a hunchback, he is a giant when it comes to understanding electricity, which is the lifeblood of your company. His subordinates, when they have a problem, always say that they will take it to the "Supreme Court," and Steinmetz is the Supreme Court. Everybody knows that Steinmetz is brilliant and that his contributions to the company have been invaluable, but as a department head, he is a bottleneck. The calculating section keeps getting larger and larger, but it doesn't seem to be producing proportionally more answers, although it never fails to deliver when the chips are down. Would the interests of General Electric best be served by

A. **retiring Steinmetz with a golden parachute and a testimonial dinner thanking him for what he has done for the company?**

B. **asking him to conduct a departmental restructuring, pointing out that there are problems within his department?**

C. **promoting him sideways into a position that allows him to pull other people's chestnuts out of the fire by solving whatever problems they find difficult?**

SOLUTIONS: *The Hunchback*

A. You retire Steinmetz with a golden parachute and a testimonial dinner thanking him for what he has done for the company. −2 points. Are you kidding? You measure your payoffs by computing how the action will make the calculating department more productive and how you will best be able to make use of Steinmetz's talents. This action is analogous to shooting the messenger who brings bad news. It is impossible that the company will be better served by retiring a man who still has not only talent but the admiration of those with whom he works. *It is more important to rearrange how you make use of an asset than to try to tailor that asset to fit into the use you have assigned.*

B. You ask him to conduct a departmental restructuring, pointing out that there are problems within his department. −1 point. This is a unique situation. It is highly probable that you have an eccentric genius in a position that should be occupied by an efficient administrator. Steinmetz may be neglecting the nuts and bolts of keeping the department running smoothly and productively, which doubtless holds no interest for him. If you suggest he restructure the department, he may not know how to go about it, and it might not be the right idea anyway.

C. You promote him sideways into a position that allows him to pull other people's chestnuts out of the fire by solving whatever problems they find difficult. 5 points. This is just the ticket. The New York Yankees faced a similar dilemma and resolved it by taking a talented pitcher who could only contribute to the team every four or five days and turning him into a first baseman who could play every day. The pitcher's name was Babe Ruth.

WHAT ACTUALLY HAPPENED

In 1913, Charles Steinmetz was removed as the head of the calculating department and made the world's first consulting engineer. In the ten years before he died, he helped by contributing significant solutions to many practical problems but concentrated on understanding lightning. He created ways to generate lightning artificially, which led to the creation of atom smashers.

Dot-Com Redux

Happy days are definitely here again for the stock market. The Middle East has simmered down substantially, the price of oil has dropped dramatically, and terrorist incidents are few, relatively minor, and far between. This is mostly good news—but you're lagging behind the pack because you've put most of the assets of the fund you manage in stock indexes, which perform as well as the market, no better and no worse. The partners at your firm are looking over your performance, and they're less than satisfied. However, you think you've seen this scenario before—it seems a lot like the end of the dot-com boom in the nineties, when everything just fell out of bed. Your judgment has generally been pretty good—which is why you're a fund manager—but age has tempered your aggressiveness. It's time to fish or cut bait. Should you

- **A.** **make the aggressive move, go along with the general feeling of the market pundits, and put a sizeable chunk of your fund into trendy stocks?**
- **B.** **stay with index funds and settle for doing what the market does?**
- **C.** **back your better judgment and convert a good portion of your assets to money-market funds to guard against the next dot-com downturn?**

SOLUTIONS: *Dot-Com Redux*

A. You make the aggressive move, go along with the general feeling of the market pundits, and put a sizeable chunk of your fund into trendy stocks. 3 points. The key point here is to avoid disaster—for you. If you adopt this alternative and the majority of the market pundits are right, you look very good and the heat will be off. If the market pundits are wrong, there will be a lot of rats going down with the ship, and no individual rat will be subject to undue scrutiny. If you're going to be a loser, it's a lot easier to hide in a crowd of losers. This worked pretty well when Wall Street tanked in 2008 and 2009, as there wasn't any giant purge of fund managers.

B. You stay with index funds and settle for doing what the market does. 5 points. This is probably the best minimax play. If the market does well, you'll also do well, although not quite as well as the aggressive fund managers, but it's awfully hard to fire a winner just because he didn't win as much as possible. If the market does badly, you'll outperform the more aggressive fund managers, and again, it's hard to fire someone who outperforms the majority of his colleagues. In either case, you manage to CYA.

C. You back your better judgment and convert a good portion of your assets to money-market funds to guard against the next dot-com downturn. 1 point. This is a bad environment to be a rugged individualist. If the market does well, you're going to be out of a job. If the market does badly, you'll be a hero both to your investors and to the fund managers—but you could have survived had you simply bought index funds. It's far better to choose a "heads you win, tails you don't lose" option than a "heads you win big, tails you lose big" alternative. *A strategy that reduces variability is a minimax strategy, and sometimes disasters can be avoided by looking for the strategy that is least affected by changing conditions.*

WEEK 4, Quiz 2

Poison Pill

Centuries ago, they knew about the effectiveness of extract from willow bark in treating pain and fever, but it was less than a century ago that aspirin was synthesized and became a staple of the medicine cabinet. However, aspirin has some undesirable side effects, notably ulcers and stomach bleeding, and your company, Johnson & Johnson, had the leading competitor to aspirin. Acetaminophen relieves pain and fever also, but without the unpleasant side effects, and under the trade name Tylenol, it contributes almost 20 percent of your annual profits. However, something has just happened that threatens to cut the sales of Tylenol to zero. It's the fall of 1982, and some sicko in Chicago has put lethal doses of cyanide in packages of Extra-Strength Tylenol. Seven people have now died, and you have a major headache on your hands that neither aspirin nor Tylenol can cure. You've pulled Tylenol off the shelves and the police are investigating, but you've got to decide the future of Tylenol. Should you

A. repackage Tylenol in the newly developed tamper-resistant gelcaps and bottle them in tamper-evident containers?

B. make Tylenol a prescription-only drug so it is no longer available over the counter?

C. wait awhile and repackage acetaminophen, an effective and widely used analgesic, under a different brand name so as to remove the Tylenol taint?

SOLUTIONS: *Poison Pill*

A. **You repackage Tylenol in the newly developed tamper-resistant gelcaps and bottle them in tamper-evident containers. 5 points.** You have two sets of payoffs to consider: restoring consumer trust in your products (for this could impact your entire product line) and restoring the profit that Tylenol has generated. Repackaging Tylenol addresses both these problems. *This is a terrific example of a Bayes' Criterion decision in which you bite a painful bullet now in order to generate the greatest amount of long-term payoffs.*

B. **You make Tylenol a prescription-only drug so it is no longer available over the counter. 1 point.** This solves one of your problems: restoring consumer trust. It's possible that you might be able to make up for the loss in profit by raising the price, but this is dangerous. Aspirin is effective and cheap. Tylenol is effective and a little more expensive, but if you make it significantly more expensive, you may drive Tylenol buyers back to aspirin or alternative analgesics.

C. **You wait awhile and repackage acetaminophen, an effective and widely used analgesic, under a different brand name so as to remove the Tylenol taint. −2 points.** It's hard to imagine a worse decision. Not only will you be losing money while Tylenol is off the shelves, when you bring it back under another name, it's going to look like a bait and switch.

WHAT ACTUALLY HAPPENED

Johnson & Johnson made the winning move, repackaging Tylenol and counting on the good sense of the consumer to realize that this response provided sufficient protection against another bizarre incident. Within a few years, Tylenol had recaptured 92 percent of its lost sales.

WEEK 4, Quiz 3

Anniversary Tea Leaves

Your fifth anniversary looms large on the horizon, and you feel that you should commemorate it appropriately by giving your wife a gift that she will treasure. Unfortunately, although there is no question that you have a really good marriage, you seem to suck big-time at reading the anniversary tea leaves. For your second anniversary, you got her an expensive dress in which you felt she would look absolutely gorgeous—she wore it once (and to be fair, she did look gorgeous) but afterward consigned it to hanging in the closet. She loves to dance, and for your fourth anniversary, you got her a series of lessons with a noted dance teacher; she took them and appeared to appreciate them (or at least your attempts to please her) but did not continue. She always seems to hit the nail on the head when she gives you something for special occasions, and you always miss the mark. What to do? Should you

A. **go with a classic, such as a huge bouquet of roses accompanied by an equally huge box of her favorite chocolates?**

B. **go with a customary anniversary gift? The traditional fifth anniversary gift is wood, and the modern fifth anniversary gift is silverware. You could "marry" the two, with a gift of silverware in a wooden presentation box.**

C. **ask her what she wants?**

SOLUTIONS: *Anniversary Tea Leaves*

A. You give her a huge bouquet of roses accompanied by an equally huge box of her favorite chocolates. −1 point. What are your payoffs here? You want to commemorate this special anniversary by showing her how much you treasure the marriage and how much you appreciate her. This gift is indeed a classic—but it's a classic "oops, tomorrow is our anniversary and I almost forgot" gift. You struck out before with the dress and the dance lessons, but at least she knows you were thinking of *her.* It's important to use the information you've acquired in making a decision.

B. You go with a customary anniversary gift. 1 point. In contrast to the "roses and chocolates" option, this at least shows you put some thought into it—but you're putting your marriage in the same category as all those other marriages that have clocked five years. *Now is the time to make use of the information you've learned about your wife, and what you've learned is that what's sauce for the goose is not necessarily sauce for the gander.*

C. You take the direct route and ask her what she wants. 5 points. Romantics may howl with dismay at this solution, but it is the hands-down winner. Your payoffs are making her happy— your previous attempts have shown thought but have not brought success. Asking her what she wants shows that you *really* care and is most likely to achieve the desired result. Get the nicest anniversary card you can find, put it in a fancy box, and inscribe it with these words: "Darling, you've given me everything I want in a marriage, and now I'd like to give you something that you really want for our anniversary, but I'm stumped. Every time I've tried to come up with something, I've missed the target. I could sure use a hint, a suggestion, or a request."

WEEK 4, Quiz 4

Conscience-Stricken

You are familiar with the saying "the more the merrier," but you are Sir Thomas More, and at the moment you are far from merry. To say the least, your career up to this point has been illustrious. You have been a successful lawyer, you authored the wildly successful satirical novel *Utopia*, you were a successful diplomat, and *then* your star began to rise! You were knighted and made a member of the Privy Council. In 1529, King Henry VIII made you lord chancellor, the first layman ever to hold that position. Unfortunately, your relationship with Henry VIII started to deteriorate, in part because of his behavior and in part because of your stalwart Catholic beliefs. Henry wanted a divorce from Catherine of Aragon, and you could not in good conscience support this challenge to the authority of the pope. In 1532, you resigned the chancellorship, and things have gone from bad to worse. Henry wants you to sign the oath of adherence to the Act of Succession, asserting that Anne Boleyn's children (not Catherine of Aragon's) have the right to the throne. If you fail to sign, you will be charged with treason and probably executed. You are caught between the frying pan of Henry's anger and the (possibly eternal) fire that awaits you if you disobey the pope. Is your best course to

A. refuse to sign the oath on the grounds that, according to your beliefs, it would jeopardize your immortal soul?

B. try to persuade Henry to reword the oath to enable you to pledge loyalty to the king?

C. sign the oath to avoid trial and possible execution?

SOLUTIONS: *Conscience-Stricken*

A. You refuse to sign the oath on the grounds that, according to your beliefs, it would jeopardize your immortal soul. 3 points. This is a situation in which as you can definitely compute your payoffs for each action. As a good Catholic, your payoffs for preserving your immortal soul by not challenging the pope are greater than your payoffs for doing what is expedient by extending your stay on Earth. As a result, the payoffs for this action dominate the payoffs for signing the oath.

B. You try to persuade Henry to reword the oath to enable you to pledge loyalty to the king. 5 points. Nice work if you can get it, and you should certainly be willing to try to find a compromise solution that will enable you to have your cake and eat it, too. *The best type of compromise is a win-win solution, which unfortunately is not always available. In such cases, there may be a compromise that increases payoffs to one party without a noticeable decrease in payoffs to the other.* You must try to make it clear to Henry that you are not being disloyal to him but that the pope represents a higher authority for a good Catholic than the king.

C. You sign the oath to avoid trial and possible execution. −1 point. While you would certainly not be the first person to choose this action when faced with such a decision, it is the wrong move from the standpoint of decision theory and your payoff scheme. Of course, the assumption is that the payoffs from saving your soul are greater than the payoffs for saving your earthly life. To a devout Roman Catholic, such as Sir Thomas More, the payoffs are clear. And so is the choice.

WHAT ACTUALLY HAPPENED

Sir Thomas More tried to persuade Henry of his loyalty, but Henry wouldn't accept a compromise solution, and so More chose the action with the highest payoffs as dictated by his conscience. He was tried for treason and executed in 1535. In 1935, four hundred years after he was beheaded, the Catholic Church officially made him a saint.

What You Can Learn from History

Other people's decisions sometimes appear inexplicable—but that's often because your payoffs are different from theirs. More knew his decision was tantamount to committing suicide, but it was not irrational. His payoffs were in the hereafter rather than the here and now.

WEEK 4, Quiz 5

Jeans Blues

Shortly after the California gold rush of 1849, Levi Strauss opened a dry goods store in San Francisco. When he was informed that the miners were having trouble finding a sturdy pair of pants, he saw an opportunity—or maybe he was just repelled by the thought of a lot of pantsless miners. At any rate, he made a pair of pants out of canvas and copper rivets—and jeans were born. Very few things say "America" like a pair of blue jeans, and a century later everyone is wearing them—cowboys, farmers, ordinary people, and movie stars like James Dean. "Levis" are synonymous with jeans. Levi Strauss, the company, formerly was privately held, but in 1971 the company went public, and now Wall Street is pushing growth as the way to boost the value of your shares. As a director in the company, you have to decide whether to grow, and if so, which way. Should you

A. **establish yourself as a clothes company by using your profitable jeans operation to fund the purchase of other lines of clothing, such as shirts?**

B. **tell Wall Street to shove it, you're doing nicely as the number-one jeans producer and intend to make sure you stay on top?**

C. **expand your product line to produce casual pants as well as jeans?**

SOLUTIONS: *Jeans Blues*

A. **You establish yourself as a clothes company by using your profitable jeans operation to fund the purchase of other lines of clothing, such as shirts. 0 points.** There's no synergy here. One of the reasons for branching out is to lend your name and credibility to closely related products. People think "jeans" when they think of Levi Strauss. Trying to push shirts as part of the brand name "Levis" could actually be counterproductive—people may stop thinking of your jeans as strongly as they do. *Failure to know who you are—and why people approve of you—often leads to poor decisions and loss of confidence; one of the reasons George W. Bush had low approval ratings is because his expensive programs were not consistent with the "Republican" brand name.*

B. **You tell Wall Street to shove it, you're doing nicely as the number-one jeans producer and intend to make sure you stay on top. 3 points.** An eminently reasonable move. You are who you are, and while you're on top of the mountain now, a mountaintop is always a precarious perch. Lose track of your corporate identity, and other jeans companies may take significant market share.

C. **You expand your product line to produce casual pants as well as jeans. 5 points.** This is your best chance at a larger piece of the apparel pie. Jeans are *really* casual pants, suitable for work in extreme conditions. Slightly dressier casual pants represent a reasonable expansionist move, as they are obviously closely related to jeans, and you aren't risking losing jeans customers through a confusing shift in corporate identity.

WHAT ACTUALLY HAPPENED

Levi Strauss initially decided to purchase diverse clothing lines, including sportswear and women's clothing. Bad move—but the failure of these purchases were buried in the increased business in jeans. Levi Strauss eventually decided to produce the Dockers brand of casual pants, which proved to be a huge success.

Empire Builder

You were the first (and so far, the only) person to conquer the world, and maybe that's why they're starting to call you Alexander the Great. After the assassination of your father, Philip of Macedon, you were surrounded by domestic enemies and threatened by rebellion on the foreign front. Nonetheless, your skill as a warrior enabled you to defeat the other Greek states, and you have just emerged triumphant in a monumental battle with your ancient foe, Persia. There are still new worlds to conquer, but equally important is the necessity of not having to reconquer the opponents you have already vanquished. If you are to achieve your dreams of empire, you need to devise a strategy for dealing with conquered territories that will not only maximize their benefit to you but will minimize the discontent that inevitably springs from being conquered. After some thought, you have constructed three alternative actions. Should you

A. **leave a garrison behind in each conquered territory that will be responsible for governing it?**

B. **establish a privileged class from the conquered population that will have the responsibility of governing in your absence?**

C. **leave a small entourage behind, which you will encourage to adopt local customs and mix with the local establishment to try to engender in the conquered territory a feeling of belonging?**

SOLUTIONS: *Empire Builder*

A. You leave a garrison behind in each conquered territory that will be responsible for governing it. 1 point. What are your payoffs? If they are to be measured strictly in terms of the plunder you can exact from a conquered territory, this might be the best action. If your payoffs are measured in terms of rebellion potential, this action is certainly going to create the hostile feelings that classically lead to rebellions.

B. You establish a privileged class from the conquered population that will have the responsibility of governing in your absence. −1 point. The payoffs for this action are dominated by the payoffs for option A. The fact that you have created a privileged class of locals will not only generate more resentment on the part of the populace, but because the governors will be natives, their loyalty will be in question if it comes down to crunch time.

C. You leave a small entourage behind, which you will encourage to adopt local customs and mix with the local establishment to try to engender in the conquered territory a feeling of belonging. 5 points. A cooperative solution that can easily be seen to generate your biggest payoffs. Although this action may not generate the maximum revenues for your empire, that's not how you are measuring your payoffs. This action has the best chance of turning a foe into an ally. What more could you want? *It's a lot better to turn a liability into an asset than simply to remove the liability.*

WHAT ACTUALLY HAPPENED

Alexander the Great was perhaps history's first and greatest specialist in the art of the hostile takeover, as evidenced by his winning choice of option C. It would have been far more difficult to hold his vast empire together in an era of primitive communications had he chosen to maximize immediately the exploitation of his conquests, which was the generally accepted merger and acquisition philosophy of the times.

What You Can Learn from History

Victory comes with a price tag, whether the victory is achieved in battle, business, or personal relations. Victory almost always engenders a certain amount of bad blood in the loser, and this is not always easy to mop up. One almost certain way to maximize the amount of bad blood is to win the same victory twice—once you have won an argument, let it rest. Women, take note.

OS Wars

For almost two decades, DOS, an acronym for disk operating system, has been the gold standard for how computers manage their programs. That's changing, and as a corporate strategist for Microsoft, you've got to figure out how to make the winds of change blow favorably. You've spent a lot of time and money creating Windows, a new operating system that has some similarities with the revolutionary method developed by Apple for their Macintosh computers in the early 1980s. However, there are some other popular operating systems out there that have received more critical accolades. You're worried about two things: Macintosh computers overtaking PCs in popularity, as only PCs can run Windows, and other operating systems becoming more popular than Windows. You've got to take decisive action, otherwise Microsoft stands a good chance of becoming a minor player on the software scene. Should you

A. buy out one of the smaller software companies that has a better operating system and incorporate it in Windows?

B. persuade computer manufacturers to install Windows on their computers so that customers can simply plug and play—or compute?

C. hold off on releasing Windows until you can produce an operating system that is as good or better than anything on the market?

SOLUTIONS: *OS Wars*

A. **You buy out one of the smaller companies that has a better operating system and incorporate it in Windows. 3 points.** This option has a good deal of potential following several criteria. You can come out with a better product (although not immediately), and you can strengthen your position as an industry leader. If you build a better mousetrap, the world will beat a path to your door.

B. **You persuade computer manufacturers to install Windows on their computers so that customers can simply plug and play—or compute. 5 points.** Or, you can make it impossible (or extremely difficult) for anyone else to sell their mousetraps. For better or for worse, good marketing strategy trumps good products. This also has the added allure of forcing the smaller companies to cave, preventing them from becoming even more of a threat in the future. *When you decide to form a coalition, you have to consider the strength of the coalition, not just how good the fit is.*

C. **You hold off on releasing Windows until you can produce an operating system that is as good or better than anything on the market. −2 points.** Not only is there no guarantee that you can produce a better operating system that doesn't infringe on someone else's patents, if you hold off, you create an impression of weakness that will not bode well for your future.

WHAT ACTUALLY HAPPENED

Microsoft chose the winning play of bundling Windows with PCs. This move gained control of that portion of the market that Apple could not penetrate and forced companies that actually had better operating systems to sell out. Even if a gambler has a mathematical advantage, he can lose his entire bankroll to a better capitalized opponent, a phenomenon known as "gambler's ruin."

OK—now it's time to see how you've done. Compute your total for the twenty-eight quizzes by adding up the weekly totals.

YOUR TOTAL	ASSESSMENT (THIS IS EDU-SPEAK FOR WHAT USED TO BE CALLED "GRADES.")
110–140	I'd be happy for you to make my decisions for me.
85–109	You're probably making pretty good decisions for yourself.
60–84	Some rereading wouldn't hurt.
35–59	I wouldn't be surprised if you're a California politician.
Less than 34	Hopefully you'll find a job advising Osama bin Laden.

239

INDEX

18